UNDRESSED

UNDRESSED

The Naked Truth about Love, Sex, and Dating

JASON ILLIAN

WARNER
Faith®

NEW YORK   BOSTON   NASHVILLE

Unless otherwise indicated, all Scripture quotations are taken from the
Holy Bible: New International Version®. NIV®. Copyright © 1973, 1978, 1984
by International Bible Society. Used by permission of Zondervan
Publishing House. All rights reserved.

Scriptures noted KJV are taken from the King James Version of the Bible.

Scripture quotations noted NASB are taken from the New American
Standard Bible®, Copyright © 1960, 1962, 1963, 1968, 1972, 1975, 1977, 1995 by
The Lockman Foundation. Used by permission.

Warner Faith
Hachette Book Group USA
1271 Avenue of the Americas
New York, NY 10020

Visit our Web site at www.warnerfaith.com.

Printed in the United States of America

First Edition: October 2006
10 9 8 7 6 5 4 3 2 1

Warner Faith and the "W" logo are trademarks of Time Warner Inc.
or an affiliated company. Used under license by Hachette
Book Group USA, which is not affiliated with Time Warner Inc.

Library of Congress Cataloging-in-Publication Data

Illian, Jason.
Undressed : the naked truth about love, sex, and dating / Jason Illian.
p. cm.
ISBN–13: 978-0-446-52674-6
ISBN–10: 0-446-52674-6
1. Sex—Religious aspects—Christianity. 2. Dating—Religious aspects—
Christianity. 3. Love—Religious aspects—Christianity. 4. Man-woman
relationships—Religious aspects—Christianity. I. Title.
BT708.I45 2006
241'.66—dc22 2006007546

To Momma "The Queen" Illian.
Your love not only gave me wings,
but it also taught me to fly.

Contents

Acknowledgments

Saying "thank you" to everyone who contributed to this book would not even begin to express my deep, heartfelt appreciation and love for their hard work and time. I truly believe that this is not *my* book, but *ours:* a collaborative effort of hearts and minds straining forward to understand the depths of true love.

First and foremost, I want to hug Lou Taylor, Robin Greenhill, and the entire team at Tri Star Sports and Entertainment for believing in me. You stepped out in faith, putting both your hearts and hands on the line, and for that I am eternally grateful. You are not only the best management team on the planet, but you are also my best friends. I desire to work with you as long as you'll have me.

Likewise, I'd like to run through the hallways of Warner Faith and high-five all those who believed in this project, including Chip MacGregor, who helped get this book off the ground. Jana Burson and Lori Quinn, thanks for spearheading the cause and solidifying the vision. Anne Goldsmith, I hope I "fleshed out" all the issues for our readers—thanks for taking my writing to the next level. To the myriad of others whom I forgot to mention by name, chalk up my forgetfulness to too many shots to the head on the gridiron.

A manly chest-bump is reserved for those godly men who helped shape my soul and who have walked with me through all seasons of life. Dad, thank you for always telling me that you loved me and encouraging me to pursue my dreams. To my brothers, Travis and Ben (a.k.a. Thor and Guido), you two are mighty warriors, and I will always tow the line with you. To Jon Sherman and Dr. Tony Evans, you have carried the torch in front of me to help guide the way. There is a special place in heaven for all of you.

I'd also like to honor those women who reflect Christ in all aspects of their lives. Marshawn Evans, Hala Saad, and Sabrina Kay redefine beauty, and it is no coincidence that you are successful at everything your hands touch. Y'all (Texan for "you guys") painted a picture of unconditional love for me, and now I won't settle for anything else. To Momma "The Queen" Illian, my limited ability to write is no match for your genius at living. You set me free while holding me close at the same time. I love you. And, "Posh" . . . well . . . let's just say that I hope our story goes on forever. . . .

Finally, I'd like to give a big shout out to all the corporate executives, bagel-store owners, church leaders, exotic dancers, valets, professional athletes, mechanics, conference attendees, fans, ex-girlfriends, coaches, waitresses, and Internet friends who have shared their stories with me. This manuscript has been a labor of love, and it is because of all of you.

Most important, thank You, Lord Jesus. May this book be a reflection of Your intentions for romantic love, and may You use it to impact millions of lives. Without Your sacrificial example on the Cross, we would be forever lost. May all glory be unto You.

Introduction

Since appearing on national television and stating that my body is not a carnival ride, I've been amused by the different responses I've received from people. Some mothers want to match me up with their daughters, and some "mothers" want to get me in a steel-caged death match. Some producers think I should land on television, and some producers think a television should land on me. Some people think I should run for office, and some people think I should run for cover. But for the most part, whether people agree with me or not, whether they like me or not, or whether they think I'm handsome or not, they respect my stand. That alone shouts volumes about our Christian faith.

One of the most interesting questions I receive is, "Since you speak on relationships and have been on a reality dating show, do you consider yourself an expert?"

I always respond from the cheap seats with the same screaming, vein-popping "*No!*" Love is the one area of life where if you walk in with all the answers, you are doomed to fail. Love isn't an equation to be figured out. It doesn't fit nicely into a twelve-step self-improvement program. It can't be planned, persuaded, plotted, or promoted. It doesn't go to the highest bidder, and it can't be bought by the richest of men. You aren't an expert on love just because you've dated, married, written a book, hosted a show, or spoken to Dr. Phil.

I'm certainly no exception. I'm just a fellow foot soldier in the trenches of romance, fighting for this thing called "love." I've dated older women, younger women, single women, divorced women, women without jobs, women without sense, and women without faith. I've waited, watched, wondered, wished, and wanted many of these magnificent creatures over the years, but I've usually stumbled and fumbled all over myself and never gotten their number. I've found that dating is like being processed in a meat packing line, I've heard guys use cheesy pickup lines, and I've learned that it is more important to draw a line than stand in line. I've whispered, "I love you," I've shouted, "I hate you," and I've realized that you can be hurt on either occasion.

I've sat on her lap, walked on her dreams, run into trouble, and even hopped into her bed. I've touched a girl's heart without touching her body, and I've touched a girl's body without touching her heart. I've kissed a woman's hand, I've kissed a woman's lips, and I've even been told to kiss a woman's butt. Some of the time I think I'm getting it right, some of the time I think I'm getting it wrong, and some of the time I'm not thinking at all.

I've been in the penthouse, jailhouse, doghouse, and out-house. I've met women in churches and in bars, and ironically, most of them believe and want the same things. I've prayed for the woman of my dreams, and I've dreamed of the woman in my prayers. I've learned to fall and fly, smile and cry, and live and die by the desires and passions of my heart.

And through it all—the memorable dances, the lonely Friday nights, the sweet love letters, and the broken engagement— God has been there guarding my heart. I may not have recognized Him at the time, but I can now see His fingerprints all over my life. Even though we often see love as a frilly sentiment, an adolescent infatuation, or an erotic dream, I still believe, deep down, that it is the boldest and most rewarding of human initiatives. Love is about people who at one and the same time can be both cruel and compassionate, barbaric and beautiful, sinners and saints, full of hope and full of despair.

In other words, it is about us.

A life under construction,
Jason Illian

UNDRESSED

1

Completely Incomplete

Being Whole While Being Torn in Half

"The pure and simple truth is rarely pure and never simple."

OSCAR WILDE

Somewhere along the way—probably between thinking that the mullet was sexy and that plaid was the new black—we began to believe that it was impossible to have a godly relationship in the *Bachelor*-watching, Gap-shopping, MTV-styling world. We began to believe that dating was just a training ground for divorce. We had to have either a satisfying relationship with Christ or a romantic relationship with a significant other. But we couldn't have both. It was an either/or dilemma. Watch either *The Oprah Winfrey Show* or *The 700 Club*. Read either *Cosmo* or the Bible. Conform to either the "kiss-dating-and-the-hope-of-a-normal-relationship-good-bye" view or the "satisfy-yourself-and-to-hell-with-everyone-else" view. There was no middle ground.

But that just doesn't seem to make sense. Why would a

good, compassionate, and faithful God instill such a strong sense of romantic love in our hearts but not give us an outlet to express it? Many of us feel the need to have an intimate relationship with our Lord and Savior *and* a romantic relationship with a significant other. Like a banjo in an orchestra, the either/or concept just doesn't sound right.

The reason it doesn't sound right is because it isn't right. It is wrong. And I don't mean kind of wrong. I mean pink-spandex, 140-decibal Marilyn Manson wrong! Our God isn't an either/or God. He is a God of both/and. He desires for you to have an intimate relationship with Him *and* a romantic relationship with another. Your heart was not designed to love God one way and your partner another. They are not mutually exclusive, but instead, divinely complementary. Romantic love is built on the precepts of God's unconditional love. You can be madly in love with another because you are madly loved by God. You can have both. In fact, Christ exemplified the strength of His both/and power by being all God *and* all human at the same time.

It's not that all of our relationships up to this point have been wrong; they just haven't necessarily been right. We have a foundation, but it is just a little shaky right now. Sex is *not* a basic human need like food, water, and shelter—I've seen a person die of malnutrition, but I've never seen a person keel over in the middle of the street because of his lack of sex. Communication is *not* the most difficult part of a relationship— the most difficult part is learning to forgive and forget when communication breaks down. Dating is *not* a training ground for divorce—it is an integral and important part of any healthy relationship. Successful couples never stop dating, even fifty years into marriage.

The problem is that in many Christian circles we've made dating one of the seven deadly sins. *The Bible doesn't talk about dating*, we argue. Well, it doesn't specifically talk about the automobile either, but you don't see people trudging their way to work on foot in the morning. Dating is about relating to other people. When you learn to relate, you learn to love. And when you learn to love others, you put yourself in a position to be loved by others. Dating is the training ground for loving, and when it is based on Christ-centered principles, you develop a fantastic, satisfying, and (dare I say it?) sexually fulfilling relationship that glorifies God.

There are fundamental truths that are evident throughout Scripture that help us navigate the rugged terrain of romance. We just need to know how to read the roadmap. But in order to go forward, you have to be willing to change how you think about relationships. Insanity is defined as doing the same thing over and over again and expecting different results, yet we continue to date in the same unproductive ways.[1] You have to be open and honest in assessing who you are and what you desire if you wish to experience a love that is unconditional. There are many ways to *fill* a life, but there are relatively few ways to *fulfill* it.

Feelin' a Little Dissed

It doesn't matter whether you are a Christian, Buddhist, Hindu, or atheist. We all want to love and be loved. But in a world where we don't know whether we are dating, wooing, courting, hanging out, flirting, sharing, living together, or just having sex, the lines blur awfully quickly. We're like a zipper on an overpacked suitcase—fighting to hold everything together and praying that our hearts don't just burst open.

If you have surfed the covers of *Playboy* and *Cosmo,* taken every personality and compatibility test written in English (and some that weren't), and sat in enough smoky bars to be mistaken for furniture, I can relate. Whether you are from New York or Knobnoster, Milwaukee or Miami, Denver or Dallas, I think it is fair to say that we've been "*dissed*" when it comes to finding love. There has been *dis*appointment and *dis*illusionment. We feel *dis*tance and *dis*belief. We are *dis*couraged and *dis*satisfied. Our hearts have been utterly *dis*mantled. We have been fooled into playing a game of musical chairs where the music is *Jaws* and the chairs are already full.

But it doesn't have to be like that. Whether you are liked, loved, or lonely, you can find a passion so soaring, so apparently transcendent that it will whisk you into love's warm embrace. If you are anything like myself—and I fear that many of you are—the love that you have experienced up to this point in your life has been prepackaged, precut, marketed, illuminated, boxed, and sold by the company with the highest budget or made by the company with the lowest bid. Great if you are trying to make a movie, but terrible if you are trying to make a life.

The love that I speak of is a "*re*" love. It wants you to *re*turn to the time when your heart was tender and your thoughts were pure. It wants to *re*store the dreams of Prince Charmings, sale-priced stilettos, fat-free chocolate bars, daily spa treatments, and engagement rings the size of large foreign fruit. It wants to *re*new your faith in a love that will last forever . . . instead of just through the first date. It wants you to *re*ceive all the things you've ever wanted but never had. This kind of love will take you back to the land of milk and honey as opposed to the land of "Remember to pick up the milk, honey!"

But in order to go there, you have to be willing to date and love differently. Our reckless whatever-works-for-me, whatever-I-can-get-out-of-this, whatever-gets-me-a-little-action approach has to stop right now. We have to stop believing that our friends have all the answers and that God has none. If you are not willing to believe that God is love—not that God has love, or gives love, but *is* love—then don't bother reading on.[2] Just take this book, prop it under the wobbly leg of your bed, and go back to doing business the old way.

Seth chose to do business the old way. I first met Seth about seven years ago in college. At the time, he was caught in the destructive cycle of sleeping with a different girl whenever the urge arose. Handsome and articulate, Seth was a catch by almost any girl's standards. But he was unhappy. Like most of us, he desired intimacy but he was foolishly substituting it with sex. When we talked about God's design for love and romance, he was curious and receptive, but it was obvious that he wasn't about to step out in faith and exercise a little self-discipline. Ironically, I ran into Seth again a couple months

ago, and you know what? He is still miserable. He has a great
job and a nice home, but what he truly desires—the heart of a
godly woman—seems like a distant dream. Even though his
dating strategy has failed time and time again, he still wants to
do things his way.

Do you really think that God would tell us about a joy that
encompasses all sorrows and a prayer that can move moun-
tains, but when it comes to talking about love and romance,
He would remain completely silent? Do you think He has just
tossed sex into our laps like a hand grenade and said, "Fiddle
with it a little while; you'll figure it out"?

If the Creator of the Universe is concerned with every hair
on your head—which for some aging singles doesn't give God
too much to worry about—I would argue that He is more than
concerned with your personal and romantic relationships. We
often forget that Christianity isn't just a religion. It isn't just a
set of rules or a list of dos and don'ts. It is a deep, intimate,
personal relationship with our Lord and Savior. Who better to
ask about relationships than the One who not only created
them but also cultivates and nurtures them to this day?

It's Not about You

If you gain nothing from this book other than discovering
that it makes a really nice coaster, please meditate on this fundamental truth—your personal relationship is not about *you*!
The *New York Times* bestseller *Men Are from Mars, Women Are
from Venus* has sold over 14 million copies worldwide, and do

you know what it says on the cover? "A Practical Guide for Improving Communication and Getting What You Want in Your Relationships." There aren't many guarantees in life, but I can promise that if your focus is on what *you* can get out of a relationship, *you* are doomed to failure. Countless couples have taken this approach, and do you know what the outcome has been? Twenty-five percent of marriages end within the first five years, and thirty-three percent end within the first ten years.[3] While there are a number of useful strategies and insights in John Gray's book, the premise is absolutely, completely, one hundred percent wrong. A successful relationship isn't about *you*.

Of course, the thought that we can get what we want out of a relationship is pretty tempting and that is why most of us buy into it. But "self" is the mortal enemy of love. Self-satisfaction, self-gratification, and self-indulgence all lead to one undeniable outcome—self-destruction. Christ came into the world not to be served, but to serve; not to accept sacrifices, but to sacrifice Himself; not to fulfill His desires, but to fulfill others'.

Think about it. When we focus on ourselves, we worry about what we can get from a relationship. But love is about giving, not taking. If you build a relationship on the premise of taking, you will literally suck the life out of your partner. You'll become a relationship leech, a parasite. And parasites cannot live on their own. They have to continue jumping from host to host to fulfill their bottomless appetite for more.

If you want to help yourself, don't focus on yourself. C. S.

Lewis once wrote, "The first demand any work of art makes upon us is surrender. Look. Listen. Receive. Get yourself out of the way."[4] If you truly and wholeheartedly want a soul mate, you are going to have to abandon the idea that the world revolves around you. Have you noticed that the only common element in every single one of your failed relationships is *you*? Surrender. Get yourself out of the way. Let God do what He does best.

If you would rather be stripped naked, dipped in honey, and cut loose on a bear reserve than go back to dating the way the rest of the world dates, you have probably fallen victim to a number of very selfish relationships. Most of us have. Mandy was a victim—she had the terrible habit of attracting those guys who emptied out not only her heart but also her bank account. Josh was a victim, too—unconsciously, he dated women who were emotionally insecure in hopes that he could help "save them." Each of them was dating people who focused solely on their own personal gratification, a recipe for heartache. Fortunately, this is not a fatal disease if we can recognize and treat it early.

The problem is that when we focus on ourselves, we can't possibly want what is best for someone else. We may want what is best for them as long as it aligns with our own personal happiness, but we won't want what is best for them if it conflicts with our desires. This isn't love—this is self-interest masquerading as mutual edification. *Love is defined by wanting God's best for someone else regardless of what that means to you.* Love is about "us" as a people, not "you" as a person.

Christ exemplified this love when He pushed aside His own personal desires and safety and died on the cross for us.

If you want a heavenly relationship, you have to be eternally minded—you can't rely on common sense alone. Common sense will give you common results. Heavenly logic is selfless. If you want to receive, give; if you want to lead, serve; if you want to stand tall, kneel down; if you want to be loved, love.

This isn't a ten-step get-better program, a personal improvement plan, or a self-help book—this is a God-help book. When you finally to come to the end of yourself, God will help.

The Fun Nazi

One of the primary reasons many of us don't pursue a deeper personal relationship with Jesus Christ is because we believe it conflicts with our heartfelt desire to be part of an exciting, intimately involved romantic relationship. We perceive Christianity to be a list of rights and wrongs, dos and don'ts, cans and can'ts, haves and have nots, especially when it comes to relationships. And let's be honest, nobody likes rules. We thoroughly enjoy our freedom, and we like having choices. Even Burger King caters to our desire to have freedom and express our individuality. Their motto is "Have It Your Way." If rules were popular, we wouldn't need police officers, detention, the FDA, or referees.

In one of the most infamous *Seinfeld* episodes of all time, "The Soup Nazi," Jerry and his ragamuffin group of friends were faced with the dilemma of whether or not to play by the rules. They craved the most delicious soup in New York, but in order to savor the succulent mulligatawny, they had to stand a certain way, walk a certain way, talk a certain way, and pay a certain way, or the cook—the one they secretly referred to as "The Soup Nazi"—would snatch the soup out of their eager hands and yell, "No soup for you!" Conform or walk away empty-handed!

Unfortunately, that is how a lot of us perceive God. We incorrectly assume that in order to obtain salvation and to enjoy the abundant life—to get "the soup"—we have to stand a certain way, walk a certain way, and talk a certain way or God will snatch the abundant life out of our hands and scream, "No fun for you!" Instead of envisioning Him as a loving father figure who wants to help guide us through the forest of life, we see Him as the Fun Nazi, the dastardly disciplinarian whose only goal is to keep us in line and stop us from living the life we've always dreamed of.

But Jesus didn't teach that. In fact, in the Sermon on the Mount, Jesus preached just the opposite.[5] In a speech called the Beatitudes—maybe, we should think of it as the "Be Attitudes"—Jesus taught us what it meant to be blessed. Being "blessed" means more than being happy. To be blessed is to experience abundant hope and joy, independent of outward circumstances. To be blessed is to experience happiness at the deepest level, a place where the heart and soul smile.

Jesus didn't say, "If you want to experience the kingdom of heaven, no kissing for you! If you want to be comforted, no snuggling for you! If you want to inherit the earth, no dating for you!" Jesus didn't say these things because God isn't the Fun Nazi. Despite popular opinion—and may I remind you that popular opinion encouraged William Hung to cut a solo album—God isn't in the business of squelching your passions. He is in the business of fulfilling them. He wants us to embrace our individuality and chase after the dreams He has etched on our souls.

But because we've taken the amazing freedom God has bestowed upon us and reduced it to a list of irrelevant, unbiblical rules, we, as Christians, have made Him out to be the Fun Nazi. Because we haven't thoroughly understood and embraced His mercy and grace, we have established unreachable standards in our personal relationships that none of us can fulfill. And it has left us disappointed and ashamed.

There is a difference between Christianity and Churchianity, and when it comes to relationships, we've been guilty of the latter. Rigid rules such as "don't date," "hang out in groups," "avoid physical contact," and "don't be romantic" are standards that have been taken to the extreme. And either extreme, whether it is too liberal or too conservative, can destroy a relationship. As the apostle Paul wrote to the church at Colossae, "Such regulations have the appearance of wisdom, with their self-imposed worship, their false humility and their harsh treatment of the body, but they lack any value in restraining sensual indulgence."[6] All these rules sound impressive, but they don't make you holy. They leave you hollow. And that is not how God designed it. Our God is a God of freedom, and He wants nothing more than to set your heart free so that love can pour into every aspect of your life.

Fenced In and Set Free

When I was ten years old, I had a friend who lived in the country. I always enjoyed going to see him because he had an enormous backyard where we could play any game imaginable. Surrounding the yard, there was a tall, sturdy wood fence that his dad had built. Even though we had all the space we could possibly need, we still thought it was unfair that there was a fence keeping us in.

A couple of years ago, I traveled home to see my friend. As we stood in the same backyard, we joked and laughed about growing up together and all the games we used to play as kids. Because we were adults (translation: older, but certainly not more mature), we decided to venture out of the backyard. You know what we found? Wolves, snakes, and big honkin' spiders! (I hate spiders.) As we rushed back to the house like a couple of frightened little girls, we both began to realize something— the fence wasn't there to keep us in; the fence was there to keep all the terrible things out.

Our Father in heaven has built a fence for us. The fence is tall and sturdy, and He has given us plenty of room to date, build relationships, and discover our passions. He hasn't locked us in a cage or tethered us to a pole to keep our romantic interests in check. In His wisdom and mercy, He allows us to explore our feelings. The fence is for our safety and protection. It is the heavenly framework within which love ought to reside and flourish. Inside of God's perfect boundaries we have the individual freedom to explore the intricacies of romance. He is not trying to keep us in—He is just trying to keep all the terrible things out.

· · ·

We've been all wrong about this God thing. Not only does He want us to fall in love—He wants us to experience a completely fulfilling, blushingly unpredictable, emotionally empowering, and recklessly romantic love that is guided not by laws, but by the Lord. By doing things our way, we haven't set ourselves free. We've limited the width and depth of love by what we think is possible. The God who *is* love and who created the heavens and the earth has a far greater imagination of what love can be than we do. And it certainly doesn't involve one-night stands, unreturned phone calls, broken promises, and shattered hearts.

Do you know why couples often long to be alone? Because when everything else is silent, they can finally enjoy intimacy with one another. But it doesn't happen until the surrounding environment is completely tranquil. Many of us have experienced a long silence in our single lives. Some of us have embraced it; many of us have endured it. For years and years, we have been alone with God and all we can hear is the quiet beating of our aching hearts. We've been listening intently for His voice, hoping that the silence would bring answers. Ironically, the silence *is* the answer. It is full of meaning and purpose. God created this silent moment to cultivate intimacy with us. He is preparing us for a love that is about to come.

Love isn't about undressing our bodies—it is about undressing our hearts. We have to strip off the layers of expectations, preconceived notions, and fears to experience a passion that will truly move us. When we do, God is free to clothe us with a love that warms our souls and our hearts.

2

Killing Jerry (Maguire, That Is)

God Completes You, You Complete You

"What lies behind us and what lies before us are tiny matters, compared to what lies within us."

RALPH WALDO EMERSON

The scene is a classic. Outwardly distraught and disturbed, Jerry Maguire (Tom Cruise) stumbles into a room of chattering, unsatisfied ladies discussing relationships. Like most men (okay . . . all of us), Jerry has done and said some rather heartless things over the last couple of months to nearly destroy a blossoming relationship. Fortunately for himself and the viewers, he has finally come to his senses. Although he has been riding a very slow steed, this sports-agent-turned-prince has finally donned his rarely used armor and has come to win back the hand of the beautiful princess.

As Jerry interrupts the meeting, Dorothy (Renée Zellweger) rises from behind the end table in fairy-tale fashion. Staring at each other across the living room, they have a moment. Jerry feels it. Dorothy feels it, too. Before Dorothy can utter a word,

Jerry begins to pour out his heart. As they verbally dance around the myriad of couches, middle-aged ladies, and cocktails, we find ourselves enamored by Jerry and his uncanny ability to share his feelings. He says he is sorry. He says he can't live without her. He says he is not walking away from this relationship. And then he says the most astounding thing . . .

"You complete me."

Dorothy is speechless. The ladies are speechless. The audience is speechless. Even *I* am speechless.

Are you freakin' kidding me?! That is ridiculous! That pseudo-romantic line is phonier than Cheese-Whiz and will kill your heart faster than a plateful of bacon! This flat-footed clown act sleeps with Dorothy, marries her because he likes her kid, talks about "shoplifting the pooty," and then interrupts ladies night to tell her that his identity as a human being is attached to their relationship. That makes me sick! If this is romantic, then Richard Simmons is a ballerina.

What's worse is that so many of us bought into it. We have come to believe that it takes the love of another human being to fulfill us, to make us complete. The reason we believe it is because we feel an emptiness inside, and we don't know how to fill it. Our hearts long for something permanent, but since we are surrounded with temporary relationships, we have become frustrated and desperate. We hold on as tightly as we can, but like sand through our fingers, human love always seems to slip away.

Our situations are different, but the pain is the same. Some of us feel a deep, internal ache when we are alone on Friday nights. Others are distracted by a gentle whisper during the work week. No matter how it surfaces, we all hear the echo of a love-shaped void that resonates with every breath. And the deeper we breathe, the quicker it feels like we are going to suffocate. Even in a crowded room we often feel alone.

This gap, this love-void, is meant to be filled, but not with romantic love. It is meant to be filled with the love of Christ. Mathematician and philosopher Blaise Pascal once eloquently stated, "There is a God-shaped void in the heart of man which can not be filled by anything except God."[1] Anything less than the patient, kind, unselfish, humble, forgiving, unconditional love of God will not suffice.

I don't fault most of us for being infected with Jerry Maguire syndrome. Through the rose-colored glasses of Hollywood, it appears that romantic love is what we desire. But if we look past the Tiffany engagement rings and the tear-jerking Hallmark commercials, we'll find that what we really desire is a love that gives us purpose, a love that unties the knots inside, a love that heals our wounds, forgives our sins, and covers our damaged hearts like a warm blanket. In other words, a perfect love.

Nothing but God's love ever completely satisfies, because the soul was created for a relationship with Him. The love-shaped void in your life is meant to be filled with God. It is upon God's perfect love that romantic love is built. When we pour God's unchanging love as the foundation—a love that does not envy, a love that does not boast, a love that is not proud, a love that is not self-seeking—we build an unshakable structure that can be home to a romantic love. But until the foundation is solid, you cannot begin to build.

A lot of us, including those of us who refer to ourselves as "Christians," have not made God our foundation. We are not comfortable in our own skin. If we were, we wouldn't be so eager to find our soul mates. We wouldn't go to church simply to meet new people or wait to follow our dreams until the right person enters our lives.

Life doesn't begin when you get married—it simply continues. That is, if you started it when you were single. Romantic relationships don't complete you—they reveal you. Like a mirror for your soul, your partner will reflect all the good and bad traits you already possess. If you are incomplete, that will become painstakingly obvious when she stands across from you and unveils your true heart. You can try to hide the emptiness, but it is impossible. You can't hide something that isn't there.

Being single is not a disease and marriage certainly isn't the cure. Some people think that marriage will alleviate all the problems that surfaced during dating. Not so. Marriage will simply magnify the problems that already exist. So, before love "has us at hello," we may want to take a long, hard, honest look at ourselves and figure out what it means to be single. It will tell us a lot about ourselves before we get married.

Staying Put

Remember what our parents taught us when we were young? In addition to reminding us not to pee on the electric fence or throw rocks at the neighbor's pit bull, they always stressed the importance of "staying put" if we got lost. I vividly remember when Mom first gave me this advice. In my mother's classic fashion, she sat at the table and used kitchen utensils to illustrate her point. The saltshaker represented me, and the pile of sugar cubes became the search party on the "kitchen table of life." After moving the saltshaker to the far edge of the table, she demonstrated how difficult it was for the sugar cubes to "find" the traveling saltshaker. "If you will just stay put," she taught, "we will find you. Stay put and let those who love you, find you."

When it comes to love and romance, we've all been lost at one point or another in the pursuit of companionship. Some of us feel lost because of the relationship we are in. Some of us feel lost because of the relationship we just left. Some of us feel lost because we've never had a real relationship. And some of us feel lost because we've switched partners more than the square dance team at the local Elks lodge. To make matters worse, most of us don't know we are lost, so we continue to frantically scramble around in the dark for something that isn't there.

If we would just be still, love would find us. Love *always* finds us. That is the very essence of true, unconditional love. For God so loved the world, He sent His one and only Son— His one and only Love—to find us and bring us into His tender embrace.[2] But it all starts when we learn to be still and know that God is exactly who He says He is. God.[3]

Please don't misunderstand me. I'm not suggesting that "staying put" means locking yourself in your bedroom, watching the Billy Graham crusade, memorizing the first five books

of the Old Testament in Hebrew, and patiently waiting for
God to miraculously bring you your prince. That's not staying
put. That's not faith, either. That's just stupid. And the majority of us have been stupid for far too long.

"Staying put" is about allowing our hearts to be still long
enough for God to share His remarkable plan for our lives. It
is about listening to the echo of emptiness within, learning the
essence of true, sacrificial, 'til-death-do-us-part love, and
applying it to our everyday relationships. God doesn't act like
Santa Claus, gift-wrapping our spouses and leaving them in
the living room for us to find after a passionate prayer. He
knows that for us to love completely, we must learn to love the
Lord first and others second.

The order is critically important. If the process doesn't
start with being still and knowing that Christ is God, you are
trying to two-step at a Jay-Z concert. It just won't work. Christ
is the source, course, and force of our lives. If you don't know
Him, you can't possibly love Him. And if you don't love Him,
you won't spend time with Him so that He can reveal to you
your true, God-given identity.

The most frustrating thing about being lost is that being
found is not in your control. It sounds obvious, but the prin-
ciple is paramount. When you are lost, you don't get to determine how long you have to remain still before love comes for
you. The Israelites were in the desert for forty years.[4] Paul was
in Arabia for three years.[5] Even Christ Himself endured the
desert for forty days so that He could clearly hear and discern
the call for His life.[6] Yet in every circumstance, love came for
them at just the right time.

Staying put requires *stillness* and *obedience*. When we are still, it is quiet enough to hear God whisper to our hearts. When we are obedient, we acknowledge that we are not in control of our love lives and that God actually does have our best interests in mind. Only when the disciples were still and alone with Jesus did He explain everything to them.[7] The challenge is that being still is about being *actively still,* not *passively moving.* And there is a difference. Many of us are just passively moving, driving through life at 100 mph with our head out the window. All we can hear is one indiscernible roar from every direction. Instead of stopping and trying to make sense of it all, we change directions, change partners, change seats, and change cars. If we would just change our focus, God would change our circumstances.

There is a reason that the Bible lists patience as the first quality of love. When we are patient, we develop a confident countenance that is built not on external circumstances but on inner contentment. Patience serves as a protection against wrongs as clothes do against cold. It is the outward manifestation of the inner belief that love is actually coming for us at the best possible time, whether or not that coincides with our original expectations.

God is in the search-and-rescue business. When you stay put, He will search your soul and rescue your heart.

Is Love a Choice?

There is something romantic about falling in love. When we hear about two people falling in love, we imagine a magical moment, a little spark, an unforgettable and unplanned experience where something happens and the couple just knows it was meant to be.

Maybe it is just an extension of a childhood dream, or a romantic fantasy derived from too many Disney films, but there is something mysterious and alluring about falling in love. "Falling" denotes being out of control, and we like the thought of love simply taking over. Because we often feel weak, the idea that love is bigger and stronger than we are is comforting. Our hearts often skip a beat when we think about love choosing us as opposed to us choosing love. It makes us feel good.

Even Plato described love as a magical, predestined act. He thought falling in love was the mutual recognition on earth of souls who have been singled out for one another in a previous and celestial existence. "We loved before we were born," he stated.[8] Sounds pretty good, doesn't it?

But is that right? Is love a magical moment, completely out of our control, or is love a conscious choice, something within our grasp?

How you answer that question will not only determine your ongoing relationship with God, but it will also determine how you will love in the future and whether that love will last.

Do you think God *wanted* to sacrifice His one and only Son? Do you think Jesus *felt* like being crucified on the cross? No, He consciously *chose* to do so because He loved us so much. He wanted to draw His imperfect people into His perfect fellowship even at the cost of His own life. At any time, Jesus could have said, "Enough! I'm not about to be mocked, deserted, flogged, beaten, spat on, dishonored, and crucified for people who don't even like Me. Let them fend for themselves." If He had said that, I wouldn't have blamed Him one bit.

But He didn't. Despite the agonizing mental and physical pain, He *chose* to die for us. Just like any other person, He had to make a decision between two options—"Do I do what is best for Me?" or "Do I do what is best for others?" Thankfully, He chose to put our best interests first. He chose to love us.

Real, unconditional, red-hot, romantic, godly love is always a *choice*. And you have to choose it every day. When you talk to a couple who has been married for twenty-five years and they are still lovey-dovey with one another, it is because they have chosen to be intimately involved in all aspects of one another's life. They have made a series of unselfish choices in which their goal was to keep the other's best interests in mind. Likewise, when you talk to a couple who has been married for twenty-five years and they have decided to get a divorce because "the flame has gone out," it is because they have chosen to give up. They have made a series of selfish choices where each individual focused only on his/herself. Either way, it's a choice.

Curious as to why most young adults want love to be magical, I asked a close-knit group of very successful corporate women what they thought. After they reflected on their previous dating experiences and talked about it, one discerning young lady, Jill, made a keen observation. She said, "I think that most people want to believe that love is magical because they think that is far more romantic than love being a choice." I responded, "But what is more romantic than a man falling to his knees and saying, 'Out of all the women in the world, I choose you. I want to spend my life with you and only you'?" It's the choice that makes love, love.

I think the reason most people want to believe that love is "magical" or "something that just happens" is because then they feel no responsibility for it. If love just "happens" to you, you can't possibly be held accountable if something goes wrong. Regardless of your involvement or circumstances, you can't be responsible for the outcome if you didn't originally set things in motion. The dangerous, tragic downside to this selfish mode of thinking is that if love can just magically "happen" to you, then it can also magically "unhappen" to you, leaving nothing but a shattered heart.

Although we may struggle to understand it, this is not a point that is debatable. God chose to love us by sacrificing His one and only Son. We choose to love one another by sacrificing our best interests for the best interests of others. This sacrificial love is the foundation, the bedrock of our faith.

Love is not a feeling—it is a commitment. Love is not an emotion—it is a choice. Love is not a frilly sentiment or a flippant attitude. It is the unselfish sacrifice of desire, the triumphant procession of hope, and the eternal stronghold of faith, which can be unselfishly wielded by the most powerful being in the universe . . . the giver.

It is your choice what to believe. Choose wisely.

Guarding Your Heart

There is a difference between breaking into Buckingham Palace, the official residence of the Queen of England, and Buck-Your-Ham brothel, the local residence of the "queen of the night." The Palace has a state-of-the-art security system, twenty-four hour video surveillance, a rotating army of the Royal Guards, and more locks and bolts than Michael Jackson's pants. The brothel has just a few rusty bars on the windows and a sliding bolt on the front door.

If you plan on breaking into the Palace, you're going to have to create an ingenious plan, consult experts in technology and military tactics, and be a ghost both entering and leaving the facility. If you plan on breaking into the brothel, you just need to make sure all the ladies are busy with paying customers. If you plan on breaking into the Palace, you'll be in the presence of royalty. If you plan on breaking into the brothel, you'll be in the presence of ruffians. If you plan on breaking into the Palace, prepare to carry away some of the greatest treasures from the Royal Collection—paintings by Rembrandt, Rubens, Vermeer, Poussin, and Canaletto, sculptures by Canova and Chantrey, one-of-a-kind examples of Sèvres porcelain, and some of the most exquisite furniture in the world. If you plan on breaking into the brothel, prepare to carry away a pocket full of one dollar bills, a squeaky old mattress, and an airborne virus.

There *is* a difference between breaking into Buckingham Palace and breaking into Buck-Your-Ham brothel. The Palace guards something of extreme value. The brothel doesn't.

Which begs the question . . . Is your heart more like the Palace or the brothel?

Our hearts—our feelings about love and romance—dictate to a great extent how we live our lives. We have no resource more precious than our hearts, which is the Holy of Holies, the place where God Himself resides. If you were a car, your heart would be the engine—it would be the power. If you were a mountain, your heart would be the peak—the place that touches the heavens. If you were a tree, your heart would be the roots—the deep, interwoven lattice of feelings, thoughts, and dreams that enable you to weather life's storms. Our heart is our key to the future, and we must learn to guard it.

At one extreme, we're guilty of treating our hearts like the brothel. We're so eager to love and be loved that we prostitute our hearts to anyone who will spend time with us. There is no security system, no night watchman, no I.D. check. We are not looking for Mr. Right—we are looking for Mr. Right Now. Addicted to the thought of falling in love, we compromise our values and ignore God's principles. What's worse is that we justify this lower standard by telling ourselves that "everyone else is doing it." When the relationship doesn't work—and it never does when we settle—we end up feeling like a sumo wrestler has walked across our heart in golf spikes.

Many of us don't shield our hearts because, deep down, we don't believe there is anything worth protecting. Consciously or unconsciously, we conclude that we have stepped over the line and out-sinned God's grace. But it is a fallacy to believe that you are unworthy of a fulfilling relationship. You are a child of God, and your past, no matter how horrific, is not being held against you. God's love is a forgiving love, and unlike most people we know, God makes no list of wrongs. Whether you have been divorced, dumped, drained, or discouraged, Jesus died on the cross to give you a second chance. And a third chance. And a fourth chance. And a hundredth chance. Whatever you have done, God will forgive you if you ask for His grace. Your slate will be wiped clean so that you can start each day with a new heart, white as the fallen snow. The question is, will you forgive yourself?

At the other extreme, the one most prevalent in Christian circles, we have grossly misinterpreted the concept of guarding our hearts. Instead of carefully defending our hearts, we have isolated them. Even though the Palace is surrounded with walls and security systems to keep intruders out, it is not completely impenetrable. Those who have legitimate business are still able to enter when they approach appropriately. Our hearts should be guarded this way as well. Instead of isolating our hearts behind impregnable barriers that admit absolutely no one, we should protect our hearts behind reasonable defenses. But because many of us are afraid of being hurt, we have decided to build only walls. No doors, no windows, no peep holes. Just walls.

"[But] to love at all is to be vulnerable," C. S. Lewis wrote. "Love anything and your heart will certainly be wrung and possibly be broken. If you want to be sure of keeping it intact, you must give your heart to no one—not even to a [pet]. Wrap it carefully round with hobbies and little luxuries; avoid all entanglements. Lock it up safely in the casket or the coffin of your selfishness. But, in that casket—safe, dark, motionless, airless, it will change. It will not be broken; it will become unbreakable, impenetrable, unredeemable."[9]

Our hearts weren't designed to live alone behind walls of fear. Our hearts were designed to face the struggles, the difficulties, and the issues of life and overcome them. Can the dating world be more painful than running a marathon in a new pair of Prada pumps? Yes. Is it possible that you will be manipulated, lied to, or burned? Absolutely. Will you get hurt and will your heart ache? Most likely.

So, what does it mean to guard your heart? It means you must learn to build *defenses,* not *walls,* around your heart. Instead of just falling for any vertebra-snapping handsome gentleman who winks at you, "stay put" until you figure out what a godly man should really look like. Instead of surrounding yourself with so-called friends who just watch you date, surround yourself with real friends who help you date. Defenses such as Godly Characteristics, accountability, and self-confidence are just three of the many skills I hope to arm you with throughout this book. For now, just know that if you don't strategically place defenses around your heart, you'll feel like taking two shots of Communion at church to help you dull the pain.

Christ should be the anchor that helps us balance our lives. We tend to gather at extremes, either constructing insurmountable barriers around our hearts that even the archangel Gabriel can't penetrate, or leaving our hearts completely

exposed to any thoughtless, mindless, ruthless, God-less beg-
gar who comes along. But your heart is a palace, not a brothel.
It is a place of royalty, not prostitution.

Dating can sometimes be rough, but it is the training
ground for loving. And if we don't learn to overcome life's
small complications and obstacles within a dating relationship, we will be completely unprepared for a lifelong commitment. If you date, you may get your heart broken. But if you
don't, you may find yourself in a far more tragic position—
your heart may become unbreakable.

"God whispers to us in our pleasures . . . but shouts in our
pains."[10] So when an exposed heart is hurt in a relationship,
our natural reaction is to run to a place where there is no
pain—into our heavenly Father's arms. Ironically, we turn to
God when we are least like God. And because He loves us so,
He consoles us, brings us comfort, relates to our pain, and
restores our strength so that we can love again.

We must learn to be *thoughtfully vulnerable,* not *recklessly
available* in our dating relationships. And that starts with
building defenses around our hearts. Our hearts cannot flourish if they are continually exposed to the harshest weather
conditions, but they need a certain amount of light and water
to grow. It is a delicate balance.

Remember, even a palace can be broken into. It just can't
be broken into *easily.* It takes thoughtful preparation, a burning desire, and wholehearted commitment to penetrate a
fortress that guards something of great value. Your heart is
something of great value. Guard it.

•   •   •

It is easy to want the perfect mate, but it is much more difficult to *be* the perfect mate. If you truly desire a mind-blowing relationship, you have to stay put long enough to decipher God's call for your life and honestly assess what gifts you bring to a partnership. Remember, half the responsibility of making a relationship work depends upon you. If you want to be desired, be desirable.

There are two primary motivators in relationships—love and fear. You can either date because you long to pour into another's life in a godly way, or you can date to avoid being alone. When you genuinely believe that your identity is found in Christ, you can approach dating with thoughtful vulnerability. There is still the risk of being hurt, but it is mitigated because you have Christ to catch you if you fall. On the other hand, if you are dating because you don't like being alone, your identity is tied to that relationship. If it crashes, your heart and your happiness go with it. You live in constant uncertainty when you date out of fear. That is no way to live.

A romantic relationship—no matter how passionate, spontaneous, or exciting—can never complete you. Only God can do that. And whether or not you develop a relationship with Christ is entirely up to you.

3

Swimming in Cement Shoes
CPR for Our Dating Lives

"To love and be loved is to feel the sun from both sides."

DAVID VISCOTT

Every summer during my high school career, I worked as a lifeguard to put a little extra money in my pocket. For the most part, I thoroughly enjoyed working on my tan and watching the scantily clad ladies from my perched seat. But like any job, there were certain responsibilities that were less than desirable. Every once in a while, one of the kids wouldn't make it to the restroom and would leave a little floating "treat" in the pool. On those occasions, I became very religious. I prayed and prayed and prayed that the manager on duty wouldn't choose me to clean up the mess. Apparently, I'm not a very righteous man because my pleading was rarely heard. Wading out in the chemical-filled water with a snorkel and flippers, I began to wonder why I didn't take the construction job instead.

There were other responsibilities that I dreaded even more. Most of the time, being a lifeguard was an easy job. But every once in a while, a life-or-death situation would occur and I would have to act quickly. If you have ever seen somebody about to drown, you know the fear and the panic. Once a person exhibits unusual struggling, he has only twenty to sixty seconds before submerging. His ability to reason shuts down, his arms and legs flail as he beats the water, and his body starts sinking like he is wearing cement shoes. When a person is in this alarmed state, he is fighting for his life. Even a well-trained rescuer can be pulled under if he doesn't approach with caution.

Unfortunately, many of us are drowning in our dating lives. Instead of cautiously wading out into the water, we have plunged right into the deep end of the dating pool and are experiencing unpredictable currents. What we thought was going to be a safe and leisurely swim has become a life-or-death situation. Frightened and fearful, we are beginning to sink. And now the clock is ticking.

If we are honest with ourselves, most of us need little orange floaties on our arms when it comes to romance—we are not very experienced. We have trouble navigating the rough waters of life on our own much less diving in after someone else who is drowning. Overconfident and unprepared, we lack much of the training needed to fight the undertow. So before we dive headfirst into shark-filled waters, it may behoove us to freshen up on a few of our strokes.

Second only to accepting Christ as your Savior and Lord,

choosing the right person to marry is critically important. If you choose unwisely, the rest of your life will be like swimming with cement shoes—you'll fight and struggle and go down slowly, or you'll accept the unbearable dead weight of your partner and sink quickly. When it comes to love and marriage, God desires nothing more than for each one of us to be equally yoked, spiritually, emotionally, intellectually and physically. And in His infinite wisdom, He has shown us how to choose a soul mate by looking for *Godly Characteristics*, *Personal Qualities*, and the infamous, indescribable *X-Factor*.

Great Things versus God Things (Godly Characteristics)

When I was twenty-six years old, I was engaged to a beautiful young lady. I know, I know, you are probably wondering what kind of escaped mental patient would commit to an ex-football player who has taken too many shots to the head. Well, I found an unsuspecting victim . . . I mean, an amazing girl . . . and after three years of dating, we decided to tie the knot.

I had been praying for this woman nearly all my life, and naturally, I was eagerly anticipating the walk down the aisle. She was intelligent, fun-loving, and charismatic. She had one of those contagious personalities that people were drawn to. She loved her family. She was stunningly beautiful. To make things even better, she liked a lot of the same things I did—

music, movies, and vacations. All the things I desired in a wife were present and accounted for.

But then something happened. One afternoon on the way to the mall, we were talking about getting married and she mentioned that she wanted to get a new vehicle. There was nothing particularly wrong with the Jeep that she had, but since she was getting a new job, we thought we could afford it. She wanted an SUV so I offered to go shopping with her. Since I had a smaller car, I thought it was a pretty good idea to have both a car and an SUV in case we needed to trade vehicles on certain days. She quickly chimed in and said, "No, I want it just to be mine and I want to get it now." Right then, I began to sink.

After being engaged for about a month, I finally realized something that had eluded me our entire relationship. She was intelligent, fun-loving, and charismatic, and those are *great things*. But those are not *God things*. I had been focusing on things of earthly value and had ignored the things of eternal value. I had been enamored with the beauty and decoration of the house, and I had paid no attention to the foundation whatsoever. I was trying to build a marriage and a life on a shaky foundation.

I was swimming in cement shoes, and I didn't even know it. In hindsight, there were many red flags to alert me—she had cheated on me, her parents didn't like my faith, my brothers didn't trust her—but I was so in love with the idea of being in love that I ignored all the warning signs. It wasn't until the current dragged me under that I realized I would never be able to breathe in the relationship.

I'm guessing that I'm not alone when it comes to choosing poorly. Most of us have dated or *are* dating the wrong person. For many believers, the only criterion for dating is whether or not he is a Christian. Instead of trying to decipher what it means to be equally yoked or to measure his heart against the fruit of the Spirit, we have dumbed it down to an elementary level—does he go to church and can he be considered a believer? We don't even care if he is actually walking with the Savior; we just want him to walk into church. That will give us enough justification for spending Friday nights making out with him.

If it sounds ridiculous, it is. And in case you can't hear, the rest of the dating world is laughing at us. We've shown about as much sense as a rabbi snacking on a ham sandwich at a bar mitzva. Our choices have absolutely nothing to do with character. They have everything to do with appearance.

Because dating can be worse than watching a single marble roll down a funnel for five hours, it is critical to understand the components of attraction and compatibility. I've spoken to hundreds of happily married couples, ranging from their mid-twenties to their mid-eighties, and nearly every couple used the following thought process as a model for their relationship, whether the decision was conscious or not.

If you want to have a successful relationship, it all starts with looking for *Godly Characteristics*. This isn't rocket science—these are simply the fruit of the Spirit recorded in the book of Galatians.[1] Just to recap for those of us who don't have this scripture memorized, the characteristics that you must have to establish a healthy long-term relationship are love, joy, peace, patience, kindness, goodness, faithfulness, gentleness, and self-control. If the person you are dating doesn't exhibit *all* of them, not just one or two—I mean, who wants a man who is good but has no self-control?!—eject immediately!

The word *character* comes from the Greek word χαρακτήρ or *carakthvr,* which means "to engrave or carve, as if in stone." If the fruit of the Spirit is not etched on his heart, don't date and certainly don't think of marrying him. These attributes are the very essence of God, and like I said, God is love. So, if you want to experience unconditional love, make sure that the person you are dating exhibits all of these characteristics.

In order to know if the fruit of the Spirit is evident in your boyfriend, you have to spend time with him. You can't simply stand across the room and stare at him, nor can you rely on hearsay. You will have to engage him in conversation and watch to see if his actions match his beliefs.

Please don't expect the fruit to be fully developed in anybody's life—we are all "under construction" and this life is a journey. But these characteristics do need to be present in the life of a person with whom you are thinking of sharing your heart.

If the fruit isn't evident, you can't train, pray, beat, counsel, or massage it into him. *You* can't change him. Only God can. Sometimes the best way to care for someone is to let him go into God's hands. Quit thinking that your relationship is the exception to the rule. It isn't.

A good way to test whether the person you are dating is a possible mate is to put his or her name in front of each aspect of the fruit of the Spirit. For example, Rob is loving, Rob is joyful, Rob is peaceful, Rob is patient, etc. Unless there is an indication that there is fruit growing in every category, he is not marriage material. Be honest with yourself.

Ninety percent of the people you date won't pass the test. And when you finally find somebody who does have all the characteristics, double-check the list with a close friend to make sure you don't have rose-colored romance goggles on.

I know what you're thinking—"Is this too much to ask for in a partner?" Absolutely not. Every person walking the face of this planet, whether they admit it or not, was designed specifically to reflect all of God's characteristics. If they don't, it is because they choose not to, and you deserve someone better than that.

Most important, make sure that *you* exhibit the complete fruit of the Spirit. If you don't, then the problem is not with the people you date, it is with you.

Perfect Imperfections (Personal Qualities)

As you have probably realized, my failed engagement was a consequence of my inability to differentiate between Godly Characteristics and Personal Qualities. While it is important to date someone who has unique qualities that you are attracted to, human qualities should never, ever supersede Godly Characteristics. If Personal Qualities are your only determining factor, be prepared for your heart to look like the aftermath of a tractor-pull when it's all said and done.

If you have been to a relationship conference or read any book on romance, you have been encouraged to write down all the Personal Qualities you want in a significant other. Theoretically, this "Must-Have" list is supposed to help guide you and remind you not to settle for anything less than your dream partner. You can review and update it periodically to make sure you are still on track.

If you have one of these Must-Have lists next to your bed or stuffed away in your Bible, I want you to take it out, walk it to the bathroom, and flush it. Or burn it. Or tear it into little pieces and use it as confetti. You don't need it anymore. It is about as useful as a sunroof in a hailstorm. The list may reflect what you want, but there is a good chance that it has very little to do with what you actually need. Besides, you can't solve matters of the heart using strategies from the head.

Most children write an exhaustive and very comprehensive Christmas list every year, including every toy and video game in the catalogue. But do most fathers buy everything on the list? No. Why? Because they know what is best for their children and want to surprise them with things they didn't even begin to think of. On Christmas morning, there is nothing more rewarding for a father than to watch his son open an unexpected gift and see the look of sheer excitement and amazement on his face. *Dad, this is awesome! I didn't know they made one of these!*

Our heavenly Father works the same way. He sees what we want, but then He goes one step further to provide what we need. If He just gave us everything we wanted, we would grow up to be spoiled, unappreciative brats like most pampered kids do. When we list the qualities we want in a mate, we are telling God that we know what is best for us. In a sense, our Must-Have lists become a list of demands—give me these qualities in a partner or I'll continue to remain single. Just curious, how is that strategy working for you so far?

Whether it is on paper or just in your head, destroy the list as quickly as possible. The good stuff never makes the list anyway. I like to refer to the good stuff as *perfect imperfections*. In *Good Will Hunting*, Will (Matt Damon) goes to counseling sessions with Sean (Robin Williams). Because Will is a genius, he has outsmarted his past counselors who have tried to get him to share his feelings. Knowing that Will likes a girl, Sean shares a story about his deceased wife.

> **Sean** *(with a coy smile on his face): My wife used to fart in her sleep. One night it was so loud it woke the dog up! She woke up and asked, "Was that you?" I said, "Yeah." I didn't have the heart to tell her!*
>
> **Will** *(almost ready to pass out laughing): She woke herself up!*
>
> Will and Sean are laughing hysterically, almost crying. After they have a few moments, Sean continues. . . .
>
> **Sean:** *My wife's been dead two years, Will, and that's the stuff I remember. It's wonderful stuff, you know? The little things like that—those are the things I miss the most. Little idiosyncrasies that only I knew about. That's*

*what made her my wife. And she had the goods on me
too. She knew all my little peccadilloes. People call these
things imperfections, but they're not. It's the good stuff.
And we get to choose who we're going to let into our weird
little worlds. You're not perfect, sport. And let me save you
the suspense, this girl you met isn't perfect either. The
question is, whether or not you're perfect for each other.
That's the whole deal—that's what intimacy is all about.*[2]

Farting in your sleep. Sneezing like a hyena. Snorting when
you laugh. Crying at coffee commercials. Never eating the
ends of chicken tenders. Constantly rearranging the pantry.
These are the things that make memories. They are perfect
imperfections, and you would never think about including
them on a Must-Have list. But they are the good stuff.

If you are intent on making a list, make a "Must-*Not*-
Have" list. Relationships are often defined not by what you
put into them, but by what you keep out of them. While the
qualities you need in a partner might not be so clear to you,
God makes it exceptionally clear what you *don't* need. You
don't need a man who wants to see you only when he is wearing beer goggles. You don't need a woman who is a gossip and
slanderer. You don't need a man who is more concerned with
making money than making meaning. You don't need a
woman who thinks shoes are more important than souls. A
Must-Not-Have list, which should be aligned with God's principles, not your own personal preferences, will remind you
that no number of great personal virtues can outweigh a few
life-threatening vices. A little bit of yeast will work through a

whole batch of dough. If you overlook the wrong personal traits in your partner, you'll be wearing the most fashionable cement Nikes at the bottom of the pool.

Peanut-Butter-and-Jelly Relationships (The X-Factor)

I love peanut-butter-and-jelly sandwiches. You would think that I would outgrow this childhood delight, but I haven't. On a beautiful spring afternoon, there is nothing better than fixing a PB&J, cutting it into squares (does anybody know the scientific reason why it tastes better in bite-sized chunks?), and brown-baggin' it to the park. It is a delicious taste that rivals any four-star restaurant.

For some mysterious reason, peanut butter and jelly taste great together. Individually, these two condiments just blend in with the other dressings in the refrigerator. But together, they are something special. Jelly is not superior to, say, mustard or mayonnaise, but when jelly is paired with peanut butter—watch out! Drooling kids coming through!

If you really think about it (and to be honest, I hope you haven't wasted nearly the time I have thinking about it), there is no substitute for a PB&J sandwich. Peanut butter and ranch doesn't sound appealing. Jelly and Italian dressing makes me want to vomit. The nuts and fruits combo just works. Peanut butter complements jelly and vice versa.

Godly relationships are like peanut-butter-and-jelly sandwiches. Each person complements the other.

When I talk about being "equally yoked" in a romantic relationship, I'm referring to the ability to complement one another and to lift one another up.[3] When we encourage one another toward love and good deeds, our relationships are pleasing to the Lord. Just like I savor a good PB&J, God delights in solid, healthy relationships.

I often hear Christians say that they can't find someone who is equally yoked, suggesting that others aren't as spiritually mature or as enlightened as they are. This attitude is arrogant and shows that the speaker has all the faith and intelligence of Spam. When you are determining whether you are equally yoked with another believer, it is not about who is greater or lesser, but about whether or not the two of you complement one another. Can you and your partner believe more, accomplish more, encourage more, and love more together than you can separately?

In the 1800s in England, during a village celebration, two farmers challenged one another to see whose horse could pull the most weight. The first farmer attached his horse to the yoke, and after a few attempts, found that his horse could pull five hundred pounds. The second farmer then attached his horse, and believe it or not, found that his horse could pull five hundred pounds as well. Unsatisfied with the tie, the farmers decided to yoke their horses together and see how much they could pull. To the amazement of the watching villagers, the horses pulled 1,250 pounds.

When you are equally yoked, you and your partner can pull more weight together than either of you can pull separately. And this isn't just a spiritual discipline. God intended for us to be equally yoked spiritually, emotionally, intellectually, and physically. While the order is important, it is just as important that you are compatible in all four categories.

Just because someone shares your spiritual convictions doesn't mean that you will be like-minded intellectually. Or that you will have a similar emotional temperament. Regardless of what you may have learned at superconservative-Bible-camp, you also have to be physically attracted to whomever you date. Just like baking a cake, all the ingredients are interdependent. If any of the elements are missing, your cake will look like pudding.

The intersection of these four attributes is hard to measure, and most of the time we simply refer to it as "chemistry," or the mysterious X-Factor. Even when the woman you are dating exhibits Godly Characteristics and has wonderful Personal Qualities, you still may not be attracted to her. The chemistry just may not be there. And whatever you do, don't try to force it. I've heard many horror stories of men and women who should have been attracted to each other but weren't, and yet they still tried to make the relationship work.

I received an e-mail from a poor soul in Boston who I half-jokingly refer to as Captain Obvious. El Capitan dated a wonderful, godly woman at Harvard who his buddies thought "rocked the Casbah." He openly admitted that he thought it was a bit strange that he felt no desire to kiss her and that he never got excited about spending time with her. But he assumed that because they shared the same faith and many of the same interests, they would grow to love one another. Two years later, they broke up and he finally realized that all he had done was deny the obvious and ruin what could have been a perfectly good friendship.

Be honest with yourself: You don't want to be *kind of* attracted to your girlfriend. You want to be deeply connected, overwhelmed with passion, and eager for the day you can cover your body in whipped cream and do a swan dive off the headboard. You should be infatuated with your girl and excited to spend time with her, whether you are going dancing or just washing dishes together. Relationships aren't always easy, but they should be exciting and unpredictable. When the infamous X-Factor is present, there will be an undeniable chemistry, and you will feel your spirit move inside of you.

The X-Factor is the place where the spiritual, emotional, intellectual, and physical attributes intersect. *X* is the Greek letter for *Chi*, which properly translated means "Christ." In essence, Christ is the meeting point where the four components come together. Romantic chemistry is ultimately determined by Christ. His ways are mysterious and unexplainable, and you can't have real chemistry with a person unless all the essential elements end at the Savior. Love isn't real love unless it comes from the source—God.

•   •   •

Attraction is a dance. It is intricate, clumsy, and confusing at first, but it is also very exciting. You may dance offbeat and step on her feet, but eventually, if the two of you hear the same music, something beautiful will develop. As John Michael Montgomery sings, "Life's a dance, you learn as you go. Sometimes you lead and sometimes you follow. Don't worry about what you don't know. Life's a dance, you learn as you go."[4]

If you have experienced the longest losing streak since Wile E. Coyote's, maybe it is because your past relationships haven't been built upon a shared set of Godly Characteristics. These are the traits that make us more like Christ, and they are the rock on which to build a lasting marriage. Once an unshakable foundation is poured, you can decide which Personal Qualities you desire in a possible spouse. For some of us, charm will be important. For others, humor. Whatever you decide, it is always wise to leave room for the unexpected—the good stuff. Because in reality, God knows our hearts better than we do and wants to bless us with a romance full of life-long memories.

In the past, I've tried to force relationships, ignoring the fact that Christ is the glue, the chemistry, the mysterious X-Factor that brings all good things together. Because we are made in His image,[5] we are naturally drawn to others who are most like Him, who pursue excellence and holiness in the spiritual, emotional, intellectual, and physical realms. I've been thankful to learn that chemistry and love are not just a matter of chance, but a matter of Christ.

A well-trained sea monkey could be taught to follow God's principles. But if you choose to ignore them, then you'd better start searching for a lengthy snorkel and a comfortable swim-suit on eBay. Because there is a good chance that the expectations and demands of the next person you date will drag you under faster than a pair of *Titanic*-labeled stilettos.

4

Sprinting with an Anchor

Dating Patiently at Full Speed

"God made woman beautiful and foolish; beautiful, that man might love her; and foolish, that she might love him."

ANONYMOUS

Relationships are like spandex—they reveal a lot about a person. How we handle relationships, especially dating, says more about our faith than a decade of sermons.

Second only to the washing machine devouring our socks, dating is a mystery to most young adults. We all have the desire to do it, but we couldn't be any less informed if we just woke up from a century-long cryogenic freeze. Some of us waltz into romance trying not to ruffle any feathers, while others of us march into relationships like Sherman through Atlanta, leaving a path of destroyed hearts in our wake. It is ironic that we spend countless hours of our youth studying math, history, and science, and yet we overlook the impact of our personal relationships, the biggest part of our lives.

Christians do many things well, but dating isn't one of

them. In fact, many of the fallacies prevalent in the dating world were created by Christians. We have been so overly zealous about modesty and purity that our faith often morphs into legalism, shaming everyone with unattainable standards of perfection. Many young adults desire a relationship with the Almighty but not at the cost of feeling guilty every single day of their lives because they long for human companionship. Even God said, "It is not good for man to be alone" and then He created Eve to be man's partner.[1] The answer to the reckless and shameless dating often seen in America today isn't found at the dogmatic, ultraconservative end of the spectrum. It is found in the balanced life, somewhere between everything and nothing, culture and faith, the place where Christ resides.

Tommy Nelson, the senior pastor at Denton Bible Church in Denton, Texas, often says, "The best way to find your mate is to run toward the Lord as fast as you can—then grab the hand of the girl running next to you." While this happens to ring true, you have to remember that a lifelong sprint requires both speed *and* perseverance, intensity *and* endurance. You have to learn how to sprint carrying an anchor. In other words, you have to learn to give a hundred percent of yourself all the time (sprinting) while patiently guarding your heart and seeking the Lord's will (carrying the anchor). It is this dynamic tension that constitutes a healthy dating relationship.

Despite what many of us have been taught, there is nothing inherently wrong with dating. But like any freedom—driving, voting, drinking—it can lead to disaster if you do it recklessly.

Even though the Bible doesn't specifically talk about dating, the Bible is a wonderful guide when it comes to interpersonal relationships. And if you think about it, dating is just one type of personal relationship. Dating gives us the opportunity to interact with a myriad of interesting people in a very unique way. Some people we will never see again, some will become friends, and some may become more. But in every instance, we have the opportunity to learn more about ourselves and about the diversity of humanity.

If you want to get different results in your dating life, you have to start by thinking differently about it. As in the other lessons that God teaches, there is a *shared responsibility* in dating. There is something for you to do *and* there is something for God to do. When God called the disciples off the Sea of Galilee, He said, "Come, follow Me, and I will make you fishers of men."[2] The "Come, follow Me" was something for *us* to do. The "I will make you" was something for *God* to do. We'll talk more about what to do in chapter 8, but for right now, realize that if you just wait for God to drop a man on your doorstep, there's a good chance you'll be marrying the postman or the pizza-delivery guy.

The purpose of dating is to find the "right one" with whom to spend the rest of your life. If you simply want to have fun, meet interesting people, or learn about yourself, don't do it within the context of dating. There is a time and place for these types of experiences, and it is called friendship. Just make friends with some people of the opposite sex if your goal is to learn and grow. Although dating sounds like an ideal way to simply shop around for Mr. Right, it is too easy to get emotionally and physically involved. And if you date with the goal of self-improvement or self-satisfaction, there is a very good chance that you're going to get hurt or you're going to hurt someone else. Dating should have a purpose—to learn who and how to love.

Every woman longs for a dashing prince to ride into her life and capture her heart. Every man longs to battle for the love of a beautiful princess. It's not just a fairy tale—God designed us that way. But how many women settle for a man whose armor doesn't shine nearly as much as his slightly balding head? And how many men come riding in on something that looks more like a Tijuana mule than a stallion? It is not that our intentions and desires are wrong. It is just that we have done a poor job of living out our values in the realm of relationships. If we truly desire to be the royalty that the Lord has created us to be and to find that special someone, then we are going to have to retrain ourselves with applicable biblical standards.

Designated Drivers

Love, or the prospect of love, is a powerful aphrodisiac. One of my friends often jokes that falling in love is like drinking five martinis on an empty stomach—you're woozy, your vision becomes blurry, and you're incapable of making a rational decision. Things that you would normally never say or do are easily justified when you are in love. But when things don't work in that relationship, many of your poor decisions come back to haunt you. You begin scratching your head and asking yourself, *Why in the world did I do that? I never act that way!*

Like alcohol, when you take a big swig of romance, it can make you do crazy things. So it is exceptionally important to have a designated driver in your love life. Or in Christian terms, an accountability partner. If you think about it, all of our notable television friends had a marching mate with whom to share both the joys and the sorrows. Batman had Robin. Gilligan had the Skipper. Scooby-Doo had Shaggy. Beavis had Butt-head. Even the Lone Ranger wasn't alone; he had Tonto. Likewise, when Christ commissioned the disciples, He told them, "Take nothing for the journey—no staff, no bag, no bread, no money, no extra tunic."[3] But He sent them out two by two. He knew that they needed each other for support and guidance.

When it comes to dating, we need to go two by two. Even if you think that you have set concrete boundaries in your physical relationship and that your morals are unshakeable, you need an accountability partner. In the process of dating, you'll be faced with a number of situations and temptations that you never anticipated. An accountability partner will help you face the facts, not just the feelings, in every situation. God is always with us, but we don't always feel His physical presence on a day-to-day basis. Having another human being there to give us perspective and balance is invaluable.

If you think you don't need an accountability partner, you

are being naïve or just plain stupid. All of the godly men and women of the Bible had people to turn to for wisdom and discernment. David had Jonathan, and later in life when Jonathan wasn't in the picture, he fell into an adulterous relationship with Bathsheba.[4] Don't be foolish and underestimate the power of this journey on which you are about to embark. Love is the boldest and most rewarding of all human initiatives, and it is the most damaging and painful when done wrong. Enlist someone to help guard your heart.

An ex-girlfriend of mine used to put it this way—blue with blue, pink with pink. In other words, men need other men for accountability and women need other women for accountability. The reason that accountability should be gender specific is because men have better insights about how men work and understand the challenges of being male. The same with women. If you try to cross the gender lines, there is a good chance that you'll end up with an accountability partner who doesn't understand your struggles. What can be even more threatening is the possibility that you will build an emotional bond with the opposite sex and may become intimately involved.

There are three *abilities* you should look for in an accountability partner: Avail*ability,* Reli*ability,* and Vulner*ability.* First of all, avail*ability.* You need to have someone who is willing to be available to you 24/7. Some of the greatest struggles in relationships happen at night and on the weekends. Your accountability partner needs to be willing to keep his cell phone and running shoes next to his bed to be ready at a moment's notice.

Not only will he be there in case of emergency, but a good partner will also schedule a regular time to talk with you every two to three weeks. You can have weekly meetings if you are working through intense issues, but I've found that getting together or talking on the phone every other week is sometimes more effective.

In every romantic relationship I've experienced, there have been moments when I was spiritually and emotionally weak . . . weak enough to have sex. When I was engaged, I shared a bed with my fiancée from time to time, thinking I could handle just sleeping in the same bed with her. I was foolish. I got to the point that I wanted her body—*only* her body. It was only by God's grace that I didn't lose my virginity. I was without accountability, and my unchecked attitudes and actions could have caused big problems. Had there been an older and wiser man there to guide me, I could have avoided much unnecessary emotional pain. Find someone who will be available to you.

Second, reli*ability.* You need to enlist someone who is reliable, a man or woman of integrity who is above reproach. Your first instinct may be to ask a family member or your best friend to hold you accountable, but I'd advise otherwise. Our family and friends are often too close to our situations to have an unbiased perspective. Moreover, they often don't want to hurt our feelings or damage the relationship. If you and your brother are accountability partners and vehemently disagree on an issue, Thanksgiving dinner is going to get awkward real quick. If at all possible, choose a discerning peer or a wiser, older man or woman who is not in your immediate circle of friends. Someone who is at arms-length is more likely to tell you the truth about your situation, even if it hurts your feelings. If you have a good accountability partner, you'll hear what you *want* to hear about fifty percent of the time. The other fifty percent of the time you'll hear what you *need* to hear.

Finally, vulner*ability*. It is absolutely critical to have someone who is willing to be vulnerable with you. You may face sexual temptations, pornography issues, emotional barriers, and spiritual depravity, and all of these issues are exceptionally sensitive. Your accountability partner must be willing to tackle the deepest heart issues and keep them just between the two of you. He also must have a compassionate and empathetic heart. The last thing you want to do is share your struggles and have someone emotionally beat you up because you are imperfect. You know that already—that is why you are seeking accountability.

Even though I hate to admit it, I need my accountability partner to ask me questions like "How are you doing physically with your girlfriend?" and "Have you viewed any pornography lately?" I need his valuable godly counsel and insight to help me overcome myself and unlock the potential that God has instilled in me.

I can't begin to stress how important it is to have at least one other person with whom you can completely bare your soul. Men, I understand that it is not always easy for us to seek out help or to admit vulnerability, but it is an essential part of being a godly man. It is when we admit that we are weak that God can pour His supernatural power into us. Ladies, likewise, it is easy to sit around and discuss relationships, but it takes a true woman of character to actually implement godly counsel and construct boundaries, both emotionally and physically. You'll find that you will attract more men when they realize that your decisions are based on integrity and character, not just circumstance.

Finding the right person to spend the rest of your life with can be an emotional and spiritual battle. Don't go into it until you know that a trusted friend has your back. If the Creator of the universe chose twelve close friends to walk with Him through his joys and sorrows, why should you be any different?

THE 5 COMMANDMENTS OF DATING

1. Thou shalt *not* group date.

Pierce my nipples. Juggle porcupines. Rip the hair off my body with duct tape. Train my cats to swim. Visit Neverland Ranch at night. Test new parachutes. Debate Paris Hilton. Wear a Speedo to church. These are all things I'd rather do than go on a group date.

When you hang out in a group, it isn't dating—it's socializing. Or mingling. Or entertaining. Whatever it is, it is not helpful. Nothing of any substance ever gets discussed in a group of co-ed friends when the intention of the get-together is to date. Emotional intimacy cannot be cultivated between two people if they are surrounded by ten of their best friends. While I'll agree that a group setting can be an excellent way to meet someone new, it is a terrible way to get to know someone's heart.

The church devised the group dating concept because it recognized the futility and dangers of how most people date in American culture. With pregnancies, diseases, and divorces on the rise, they wanted to protect their flock from having similar heart-wrenching results. I can appreciate their intentions, but going from one extreme to another has not alleviated our problems. It has just given most singles a whole new set of issues to deal with—loneliness, despair, and confusion ranking at the top of the list.

Besides, fairy tales never begin with "*A group of knights gathered together to fight for a handful of maidens, only later to decide who rescues who.*" Romantic stories are never written that way because that doesn't speak to our hearts. It is only when one knight takes a calculated risk and battles for the hand of a beautiful princess that we see true commitment and intimacy. And we long for this in our own lives.

One of the biggest problems with group dating is that it allows men to be passive. In a group setting, men can shun accountability and responsibility. They don't have to make any plans because someone else will. They don't have to be responsible for anything because it is easy to disperse ownership with others involved. And they don't have to ask any one girl out because they can enjoy all of them at the same time!

Men don't have to be proactive leaders—they can simply be pack hunters.

Unfortunately, marriage is not a group outing. When a couple finally decides to tie the knot, many men are unprepared to handle the decisions and responsibilities that come with leading a family. Cassandra and Mike, a very quiet but thoughtful couple in their mid-thirties, recently approached me at O'Hare International Airport in Chicago and thanked me for a couple of articles I had written. They told me that they had been married for eight years and that the first four years were the roughest of their lives. Mike said that he dated Cassandra in a group environment like their church suggested, but once they got hitched, he struggled with leading his new family. And they weren't alone. He named at least five other couples in their church where the men were shutting down, frustrated with their spiritual and emotional responsibilities.

One-on-one dating is the training ground that men desperately need to learn how to lead. Men are naturally more reserved when it comes to emotional and spiritual development, and their growth is slowed even more when they can mask it in a group setting. On an individual date, however, open discussions can go to deeper levels and men have to think through what they really believe. Men learn perseverance by being rejected, strength by battling for a woman's heart, and initiative by asking a beauty on a date.

Women often ask if it is acceptable for them to ask a man out on a date. I usually respond, "Do you want to lead this relationship or would you like him to lead?" If you are content with a man who takes no initiative, has a Jell-O spine, and is on track to be a passive, beer-drinking, church-skipping couch potato, feel free to ask away. But if you want a man who is going to be the leader in a relationship, it will behoove you to let him ask. If a man can't find the courage to ask you out to a simple dinner, do you really want to build a future with him?

As long as women continue to ask men out on dates—and in essence, take the lead in the relationship—men will continue to be passive. It is not that women are incapable or unqualified to lead a relationship. That is far from the case. It is just that women have a natural instinct to support and encourage while men have a habit of becoming sedentary and inactive when in a supporting role. Besides, women deserve to be treated with a level of respect and care by men. It is not just chivalry—it is called servant-leadership. If a woman wants to be noticed by a man, there are plenty of ways to do it without asking him out on a date, and I'll highlight a few in chapter 8.

There is another downside to group dating that often gets overlooked. Herd mentality. When young adults get together in groups to try to develop romance, everybody is in everybody else's business. Instead of dispersing the pressure to act one way or another, the pressure mounts. When two people in the group finally do connect, they often break away from their friends to escape the gossip and preconceived notions. We've learned the hard way that the only thing more dangerous than a misguided individual is a misguided group. Never underestimate the power of stupid people in large groups.

Single Christian groups also develop an "it's-about-us"

attitude. They are not very welcoming to new people or ideas. It is as if the people in the group believe they have earned the right to be the first person to get married because they have waited around the longest. If a new person does happen to join the ranks, he is usually enthusiastically accepted by the opposite sex—like a T-bone is enthusiastically accepted by a pack of famished wolves—and snubbed by the same sex. Because he is just one more single mouth to feed at a table that many believe is already short of good food, he is usually not a very welcome visitor.

Are one-on-one dates more intimate? Yes. But isn't that the point? Aren't we trying to get to know someone's heart to see if we can develop a romance? Group dating doesn't allow this. You certainly have to be more mature to handle an individual date and the things that may develop from it. But that is what makes it so exciting. Men enjoy the challenge of battling for a heart they think is worth fighting for, and women exude confidence when they realize their heart is a treasure.

2. Thou shalt *commit* to the fight.

The normal model of male-female relationships is quite simple—you are either dating or you are not dating. But the current Christian model is quite different. Perhaps we got held underwater a little too long during baptism, but our model looks like this: become friends, hang out, get to know one another, see where it goes, talk about possibly getting involved, discuss the north wind and how it may affect the relationship, talk to the youth pastor about it, pray about it, fast over it, court (which may mean dating), date (which may mean courting), and finally, date. Instead of having or not having a romance, we add a million meaningless micro-steps which muddy the already difficult waters.

So, to set the record straight, you are either dating or you are not dating. Commit to one side or the other. There is nothing in between. There is nothing overly spiritual or holy about camping somewhere between friendship and intimacy. In fact, when you attempt to know someone's heart without committing anything to them, you are doing them a terrible disservice. I have seen droves of well-meaning Christian men break young women's hearts because they stole intimate moments from a girl while committing nothing to the relationship. It's called emotional promiscuity. I've done it myself more than once.

For those struggling to define dating—which are most church-attending adults—dating is getting to know somebody else *exclusively.* It is purposeful intimacy with personal commitment. Many pastors substitute the word *courting* for *dating,* but I think this is a misnomer and very dangerous. According to Webster, courting is "wooing, working, and trying to gain the affection of another through attention or flattery." But you shouldn't have to persuade or entice someone to spend time with you. Courting has the connotation that the relationship is *definitely* leading to marriage, putting undo stress on the couple. Women often think that if they are being courted, they are guaranteed a proposal. But that is not necessarily the case. While you can hope the relationship leads to marriage, courtship is no guarantee that the man will get down on his knee.

Conversely, dating is about committing yourself to a developing, exclusive relationship to determine if your partner can be your soul mate. Dating doesn't hold any preconceived notions about what can or should be expected in a relationship. As Christians, we don't need a different word to explain our romances. All people, regardless of their belief system, long to love and be loved, and we can share in this pursuit when we share in their struggles. We don't need to reword dating—we just need to do it better than everyone else.

The tricky part is figuring out when dating actually starts. Is it the first kiss? Is it the define-the-relationship talk? Is it after x-number of dates? After talking to hundreds of couples, I've learned something humorous (and sad) about many Christian relationships: Many women are dating men who don't know they are dating.

Dating often begins for a woman when the man builds an emotional bond with her. This can be accomplished through intimate conversation or quality time together. On the other hand, men often equate dating to the physical aspect of the relationship. Whether it is a kiss or something more, men often don't think they are "in" a relationship until they have displayed some level of physical affection.

To reconcile these bipolar views, there is only one solution—communicate. Some of your dating relationships will begin at the first kiss and others will begin after you have talked about it. Neither side is completely right, but neither side is completely wrong either. If intimacy is taking place on a regular basis, then dating has begun, whether or not you have officially defined it. A few telltale signs that you are dating but you don't know you're dating include regular late-night phone calls, flirtatious e-mails, recurring daydreams of the other person, continuous Starbucks dates, and extra prepping before seeing one another.

I got to observe this confusion firsthand while speaking at a university recently. To prove a point about effective communication, I asked for three volunteer couples from the crowd. I saw a girl's hand waving in the front and asked her and her boyfriend to come forward. As they were walking toward the stage, I saw a look of confusion on his face. When I asked him how long they had been dating, he said, "Uh, I didn't know we were dating." Shocked, the girl quickly blurted out, "We've been dating for three months!"

If you are not sure whether or not you are dating, discuss it. If she or he hesitates or tries to stay in that awkward middle ground, jump from the moving train immediately. You are headed for disaster. You can't bounce in and out of "the friend zone" like Tigger on crack. You are either dating or you are not—make a choice.

3. Thou shalt expect *nothing.*

The number-one reason men don't want to commit to a relationship is because the only thing higher than a woman's heels on a first date is her expectations. If you think that the next guy has to be "the one," don't be surprised if he doesn't call you again. If you start talking about your dream wedding, his short trip to the restroom may detour out the back door. While many guys seem confident on the outside, most of us are still trembling little boys on the inside trying to understand this thing called love.

Expectations are cancer to a new relationship. The author, Erich Fromm, said it eloquently in his best-selling book *The Art of Loving* when he stated, "In love, if one expects nothing and asks nothing, he can never be deceived or disappointed. It is only when love demands that it brings pain."[5] We are all guilty of bringing unreasonable expectations into a relationship, even more so as followers of Christ. Because Christ was perfect, many of us expect our Christian partners to be perfect as well. But assumptions and expectations are roadblocks to finding out about the heart of the person sitting across the candlelit table.

My last relationship was with a single mother who has a ten-year-old son. If I had held some preconceived notions about dating a divorced woman, I would have missed out on eight wonderful months of dating and romance. I've always wanted a family, and while dating this beautiful girl, I watched her be a loving mother on a daily basis. I want that. I *need* that. I would have missed that had I held expectations that God had someone different for me. I don't completely know the type of person I'll marry, and if you are honest with yourself, you don't know either.

Always give yourself margin in a relationship, especially at the beginning. When I refer to margin, I'm talking about creating extra space between your hopes and reality, much like the space between the words and the edge of a book. Don't lower your standards—just give everybody the benefit of the doubt and give God room to work. When we get around the opposite sex, very rarely do we say and do exactly what we mean. The butterflies in our stomach often make us alter our predetermined plan.

Couples often talk about "love at first sight." Of course, the couples that talk about this are the ones who actually fulfill the prophecy. You never hear a person talk about "love at first sight" when the relationship doesn't work. I happen to believe that at first sight, you can only fall in love with the idea of that type of person, not the actual person himself. It takes seasons of life, intimate moments, difficult obstacles, and unwavering faith to really fall in love with someone.

When you first start seeing someone, give yourself three to four dates to decide whether or not you want to date him exclusively. Even if you think you know after the first date, give him time to realize how wonderful you are as well. Desperation is an ugly suit, and you certainly don't want to wear it on your first date, Cinderella. Unless there is excessive physical contact (not incidental—if he brushes your leg as he gets up to use the restroom that doesn't count) or verbal commitment on the first couple of dates, both individuals should have three to four dates to decide if they want to commit to an exclusive relationship.

Ideally, the man should address the issue of dating, but if he hasn't initiated the conversation after the allotted four dates, feel free to bring it up, ladies. Ask an open-ended question along the lines of, "What kind of relationship do you see us developing?" or "Where do you see our friendship going?"

Regardless of who brings it up, if the other person wavers and doesn't commit to getting to know you and only you, move on. You deserve better.

4. Thou shalt be *patient.*

Too many young Christian couples bolt out of the starting gate like they are being chased by a rabid dog. They are so excited about their new relationship that they often confuse marriage as the end of the race, when in reality, it is merely the beginning. Their passion is redlining, but their patience is still in neutral. They are sprinting toward love, but they are not carrying the anchor that will help them see all the obstacles along the way.

It is ironic that the churched, those who claim to understand the fullness of Christ's love, are often even more in a hurry than the unchurched to get hitched. How many times do you hear of young couples meeting, dating, and marrying all within a six- to twelve-month span? Since the divorce rate is as high among Christians as it is among non-Christians,[6] this tells us one of two things: (1) We preach the concept of patience, but we don't actually practice it; *or,* (2) we don't really understand the depth of true love. Why are we in such a hurry to meet, greet, eat, and feel each other's body heat?

After a church service in Texas, a handsome young stud approached me and said, "You saved me ten thousand dollars." Of course, I had no idea what he was talking about, but I joked that I'd be happy to split it with him fifty-fifty. Confident and debonair, he said that he had heard me speak two years earlier about love and patience while he was still in college. At the time, he had just bought a diamond ring for his girlfriend of seven months. After the talk, he prayed about proposing to her and decided to wait a couple of months before popping the question. And he was thankful that he did. Apparently, when she didn't get the ring as early as expected, she threw a fit and her true colors began to show. Within a month, they weren't even dating anymore. (On a side note, I've still yet to see a penny in the whole deal.)

Above all things, unconditional love is patient. When you experience a fresh and exciting new romance, you take a big swig of dumb-dumb juice. In all other instances, you would think rationally and logically, but when Cupid's arrow hits you in the backside, you begin to have outlandish visions of grandeur and romance. Everything is wonderful because "he likes me." A hoodlum could break into your house, steal your favorite stilettos, eat the last piece of chocolate cake, kick your dog, and leave the toilet seat up, and it wouldn't bother you. Normally, you would have this guy tethered to a moving truck and dragged across hot asphalt for even eying your chocolate cake. The prospect of love makes you dumb-dumb.

To combat dumb-dumb syndrome, the best medicine is patience. In Paul's letter to the Corinthians, he was adamant about saying "love is patient" first.[7] He wanted the young Corinthian believers to understand that God's perfect plan is mysterious, and the best way to decipher an enigmatic plan is to give it time. While you may *feel* that your partner possesses all aspects of the fruit of the Spirit, your *feelings* can be deceiving. The best way to check somebody's true intentions is to see if their actions match their words.

No matter how much you love someone, there is no substitute for life's experiences. Walking through different seasons of life with your partner is an invaluable indicator of how he will handle the unpredictable moments of marriage. Remember, a tree is recognized by its fruit, and the only way to see if the tree will produce fruit is to observe it over many seasons. Nearly every relationship I've experienced has hit an inflection point at both the six- and twelve-month marks. While there is no specific research suggesting why these time frames might be significant, they may be indicators of how your loved one is changing, growing, and developing. Take the time to get to know him thoroughly. If you are planning on being married for the next seventy-five years of your life, a couple more months of dating certainly won't hurt you.

To use my last relationship with the single mother as an example again, how we communicated with one another began to change at about the six-month mark. Up to that point, we both filtered our thoughts and used an extra level of caution when approaching a sensitive subject. We didn't do it to avoid speaking the truth or broaching controversial issues. We did it because we cared for one another and didn't want to hurt each other's feelings. As I mentioned earlier, young relationships are fragile and need to be handled with the utmost care. However, when we finally began honestly talking about sensitive issues, we realized that we had very different expectations on what our future family could look like. She desired a husband who could work a nine-to-five job and spend nights and weekends with the family. I, too, desire a family, but understand that my career will sometimes take me away from home for significant periods of time. After talking about it for a couple of months, we realized that even though we both loved the Lord, we were heading down two very different paths. Had we rushed into a marriage because things "felt" right or because all the boxes were checked on a Must-Have list, we would now be facing some serious marital problems. Exercising a little patience—and communicating openly and honestly with each other—saved us from much emotional pain.

If we are really honest with ourselves, the reason that most of us are impatient is because we don't want the person we are dating to get away. We are simply afraid of being alone. But is that love or is that self-interest posing as love? When I get discouraged about my love life, I remember one thing—there are over six billion people in the world and I need only one. God is more than capable of finding me the perfect mate among that many choices.

5. Thou shalt always *follow the King.*

When we are confused in our relationships, we often get this counsel from our family and friends—"just follow your heart." While our loved ones mean well, this advice is a little misguided. Our hearts—our feelings, thoughts, and emotions—are usually the very things that got us in trouble in the first place. Our hearts have very limited foresight and are easily shaken by circumstances. As the prophet Jeremiah wisely noted, "Our hearts are deceitful above all things and beyond cure. Who can understand [them]?"[8] Instead of simply submitting to our feelings and emotions, it is more important to follow the passion and direction that the Lord instills in us. Why follow your heart when you can follow the Creator of your heart? If your dream is to one day find a prince, doesn't it make more sense to follow a King and learn what princes are made of?

I recently overheard an interesting conversation at a local bar while visiting one of my bartender friends. As in most pubs, groups of men often come in looking for groups of women. This night was no different. As I was catching up with my buddy, a couple of beautiful ladies sat at the table behind me. It wasn't long before a couple of gentlemen—I use the term loosely—approached their table and started a conversation. Within five minutes, one of the girls and one of guys got up to go shoot pool. But the other couple sat at the table and talked. Now, I've been around some pretty eager guys, but this guy wins the prize for hustling a girl for her phone number. Calm and collected, she denied him this small request for over half an hour. Finally, he got frustrated and asked, "What does it take to win your heart?!"

Without skipping a beat, she said, "Don't come to me asking for my heart. I gave my heart to the Lord a long time ago."

Profound. Powerful. True. Not the kind of comment you usually hear between cheers and beers. But she was absolutely right. Had the guy had an ounce of sense, he would have realized that she wasn't denying him; she was simply reminding him where he needed to refocus his efforts. On the Lord.

Many of us need that simple reminder because we all have a choice to make. We can either take love into our own hands and try to decipher between the millions of potential mates, or we can hand our hearts over to the Lord and trust that He who is Love will act in our best interest. Stated another way, we can either do it ourselves or we can ask the Creator of Relationships for a little help. I've tried it on my own and have been humbled on more than one occasion. As for me and my heart, we will follow the King.

. . .

Although it flies in the face of most Christian thought, you have to date if you want to learn how to relate romantically to the opposite sex. Dating is not training grounds for divorce, but bad dating is. If you don't "sprint carrying an anchor" and abide by the five commandments of dating, there is a good chance that you'll be picking up the pieces of your heart with a Hoover. Remember, lasting relationships develop when two people, equally yoked spiritually, emotionally, intellectually, and physically, start running toward Christ's light and somewhere along the way begin to hold hands.

The key to meeting the right people is not worrying about meeting the right people. Simply go out and fulfill the Great Commission—"Go and make disciples of the nations."[9] It is not by coincidence that when you are constantly meeting new people opportunities to date develop. When you meet a new person, don't size him up or decide whether or not he is dating material based on the first conversation. Just be genuinely interested in him as a person, and you'll be wonderfully surprised at what develops. Our goal should be not to search for romantic relationships but, as Jesus exemplified, to build friendships. It is through these friendships and these shared experiences that the greatest romances are birthed.

And don't forget, have fun. People who enjoy life always attract other people who enjoy life.

5

Walking Back to the Castle
Breaking Up with Dignity

"Take hold lightly; let go lightly. This is one of the great secrets of felicity in love."
SPANISH PROVERB

There's a good chance you will someday find yourself riding off into the distance when you realize that you are on the wrong horse. The prince of your dreams may not be quite as noble as you originally hoped, and you will have to figure out how to dismount a galloping steed with dignity.

Although most people avoid the issue, breaking up is a significant part of dating. If you don't ever want to break up, don't date. Most of us will date, to one degree or another, at least six to eight people during our lifetime. That means that you will have to end at least five relationships before finding the right one. How you handle each breakup will reveal more about yourself than a month of MRIs.

The number-one reason many Christians want to "kiss dating good-bye" is because they are afraid of breaking up.

They falsely assume that one of the core tenets of our faith is "not getting our feelings hurt and not hurting other people's feelings." While it is a sensitive issue that needs to be handled with much care and consideration, we actually do people a greater disservice when we stay in a mediocre relationship. Christ never fretted over hurting other people's feelings. In fact, much of what He preached offended the religious elite at the time. He was concerned only with the Truth and acting it out in Love. And if the truth of the matter is that you are in a relationship that is not mutually fulfilling and God-honoring, you need to take the necessary steps to dissolve it. Like Christ, we should be concerned with making decisions that urge all parties toward holiness, not just happiness.

Whether you are the dumper or the dumpee, you need to realize that most relationships end poorly. That is why you break up, because things aren't going well. If it was going well, you wouldn't break up! While it doesn't have to end with screaming and yelling, you do need to be prepared to handle a less-than-ideal situation. The longer you date, the more you invest, the harder it will be to sever a relationship. But when you finally realize you are with the wrong person, break it off immediately. The longer you delay, the more agonizing it will be.

It is easy to become bitter and angry at the end of a relationship—if you go through this phase, understand that it is completely natural. You just had your feelings hurt, the future that you had envisioned dissolved quicker than the Bobby Brown Reunion Tour, and to top things off, you are single again. It is frustrating, and it is difficult. But it is temporary. No matter how bad it seems—and at the time it will *seem* like the end of the world—this too will pass. God promises that He "has plans to prosper us and not to harm us, plans to give us hope and a future."[1]

Relationships require a certain amount of discomfort and pain. It is part of the growth process. If you decide to date, you will eventually get hurt. But life's most valuable lessons often occur in the midst of our greatest pain. The greenest grass is found in the field that receives the most rain. You will experience your greatest emotional and spiritual growth on the heels of a devastating breakup. It is when we are least like God that we feel the need to run to Him for protection and strength. Each time you end a relationship, your heart will break just a little bit more. But surprisingly, that heartbreak can actually increase your ability to love deeper and deeper. God uses each broken relationship in different and mysterious ways to guide you toward the person of your dreams.

An entire book could be written about the complexities of a broken romance, but I just want to share three simple strategies for ending a relationship with dignity.

THE **3** COMMANDMENTS FOR BREAKING UP

1. Thou shalt *not* use God as an excuse.

As I was walking into my apartment complex, a sobbing girl ran down the stairs and nearly bowled me over. Bending over to pick up the can of refried beans I had dropped trying to avoid the head-on collision, I realized that the distraught woman was the girlfriend of my next-door neighbor, Trent. Concerned, I knocked on Trent's door and asked if everything was okay. He said that they had just broken up. I asked him what he said that made her so upset. He said, "I don't know. I just told her that I had been praying about it and that the Lord told me we shouldn't be together." Right then, I wanted to beat Trent purple with my grocery bag full of Pop Tarts and banana-nut yogurt.

Christ should be the *reason* for our actions, but He should never be the *excuse.* How many times have you heard a Christian say, "I've prayed about this, and . . . ," or "God told me that we shouldn't be together anymore," or "I feel convicted by the Holy Spirit to blah, blah, blah"? Let me scream this from the upper deck: *You* got yourself into this relationship—*you* need to get yourself out! Don't blame God! We need to start taking *personal responsibility* for our actions. Using God as an "easy out" is completely inappropriate. It makes our faith look exceptionally shallow and contradicts the true love of Christ.

God did not make you date her. God did not make you kiss her. And God certainly did not make you break up with her. Take responsibility for your decisions and do not blame the end on prayer or anything else. It is ironic how we lean more toward predestination than free will when it comes to calling it quits—we say something ridiculous like *"we just weren't meant to be."*

The biggest problem with using God as a defense is that it

leaves no room for a counter response. It makes one person look completely right and the other person look completely wrong, and that is never the case. A dating relationship is a partnership, and every issue that develops is a joint problem. If one person doesn't want to be part of the romance any-more, it doesn't alleviate any of his responsibility for the cur-rent situation. The only time you can tell the person you are breaking up with that "God told me we should not see each other any more" is when He actually appears to you in visual form, says those exact words in proper English, and leaves the phrase etched in a stone tablet as the eleventh commandment.

I'm not saying that you won't be prompted by the Holy Spirit (which most people call their "gut feeling" or "instinct") to sever a relationship as Trent was. But if God intends for your girlfriend to feel the same prompting, He'll give it to her Himself. He loves both of you equally, and He doesn't need you to relay the message for Him. When you start speaking on God's behalf on an issue that affects both parties jointly, the message tends to come across as an excuse. To the listener, it simply sounds like you are trying to shirk personal responsi-bility for ending the romance and are avoiding the real reason why you don't want to stay together.

The discussion that takes place at the end of a relationship should focus on *why* you are breaking up, not on *Who* may have prompted you to break up. Ending a relationship is a personal decision, and your conversation should say more about you than about God. Whether you and your partner don't share the same Godly Characteristics, Personal Qualities, or the X-Factor, you still need to speak honestly about your reason for calling it quits.

Felicia handled the end of her two-year romance with Juan very well. Throughout the relationship, Felicia had expressed concern about the level of trust they shared. Felicia understood that Juan needed to have "guys' nights" and supported him when he wanted to hang out with his buddies from time to time. But Juan didn't reciprocate. He didn't like it when Felicia spent time with her girlfriends. He was very possessive and often suspicious about how she acted when he wasn't there, even though Felicia had given him no reason to believe she would ever cheat on him.

When things didn't get better, Felicia knew she had to end the relationship. She didn't want to because they had invested a significant amount of time and energy, but in her heart of hearts, she believed God's unconditional love encompassed a deep level of trust. Instead of telling Juan that "God told her" that they should break up or that she "had been praying about it," she said, "Juan, I just don't think we have the trust we need to build a lifelong relationship. We've talked about this many times, but we still continue to argue over it. I think it would be best if we end this relationship now before we really hurt one another."

While "the talk" was still very difficult, Felicia did a good job focusing on the main issue—trust—and even citing a few examples. They didn't need to have a long, drawn-out discussion about who said what to whom because there had been ongoing communication about the issue. Felicia could have made it a God issue by comparing Juan's shortcomings to different parts of Scripture, but she was wise enough not to judge. She simply stated the truth about why they shouldn't be together and didn't complicate the situation with harbored resentments and personal attacks. She gave Juan space to talk to God about the details himself.

When you have heartfelt conversations that include both personal and spiritual topics, it is wise to use the qualifiers "I feel," "I think," and "I believe" in conversation. You aren't speaking for God—you are sharing your feelings about how God is leading your life.

If you are like Juan and are on the receiving end of "the talk," try not to get entangled in the details or get too emotional. Simply try to understand why your partner doesn't want to be together anymore and take the rest to God. You will never, *ever*, find intellectual closure in the final conversation. Real closure comes months or years after the relationship has ended, when you've been granted the gift of hindsight to see what God was doing with your life. Every question you ask during the breakup will provide a bottomless answer with ten other questions embedded in it. The more questions you ask, the more miserable you will feel because the more confused you will be. Besides, sometimes God allows a romantic relationship to end to give you something much, much better.

If you continue to drill the person trying to break up with you, you will make him do one of two things—*lie* or *hurt your feelings*, neither of which is beneficial. Besides, does it really matter why he doesn't want to be with you? If he gives you a shallow reason, are you going to say, "Nope, bad answer. We're staying together whether you like it or not!" You don't want to be with someone who isn't wholeheartedly enamored with your presence and your heart. You are a child of God, and you deserve nothing less than the full measure of love.

Breaking up is a painful, heart-wrenching situation wrought with emotions. If you want to act in a godly manner during the process, you have to make a pre-game decision about how you will handle the breakup. Before you ever go into a relationship, make it a point to know how you will carefully handle another's heart if you determine that you don't have a future together. I'm not suggesting that you plan each breakup before you start dating. I'm simply saying that you need to fully understand how God would have us navigate this sensitive and emotional situation. This is a great time to lean on your accountability partner for an unbiased viewpoint.

Most of the time, it's not *what* you say, but *how* you say it that makes a difference. Just try not to use God or prayer as an excuse. Take personal responsibility for your decision and be honest about your feelings. Simply listen with compassion, speak in truth, and act in love and grace.

2. Thou shalt kill the horse, not the rider.

When you break up, you need to kill the horse galloping off into the distance, not the rider. In other words, it's the relationship, not your partner, that you are trying to end. There is nothing physically, emotionally, or spiritually wrong with the other person that makes her unlovable, and you have no right to make her feel like there is. Most of the time, people simply don't complement one another. If you claim to be a follower of Christ, don't target the other person by sharing partial truths or resentments. Relationships can be good or bad, but people are not completely good or bad. The worst possible girlfriend will still have some admirable and lovable traits. That is why you started dating her in the first place.

Even if the girl you are dating has more issues than a yearly subscription to *Sports Illustrated,* try to focus on the relationship and your part in the collapse. There has never been a romantic relationship where one person held sole responsibility for its ending. Even in situations where one person has been unfaithful, the other party most likely has some fraction of responsibility in the overall relationship. It is virtually impossible to be Christ-like in every situation. There is wisdom in simply letting the other person know your reasons for calling it quits, as devoid of emotions as possible, and moving on.

When you are absolutely, positively, one hundred percent sure that you're ready to drop the relationship, make sure that you *kill* the horse—don't just *wound* it. You can't get off the horse until it comes to a complete stop and that won't happen if you continue to feed it hope. Many relationships don't die quick and painlessly—they slowly bleed to death as the horse limps off into the distance. Jerry Seinfeld often jokes, "Do it like a Band-Aid. Rip it off!" Instead of just telling our partners that we don't want to date anymore, many of us decide to stop calling, attending events, and showing affection. We simply stop nourishing our relationships and the cause of death is not willful termination, but careless neglect. You owe it to the other person to address the issues face-to-face and handle whatever consequences come with it.

I can name a handful of breakups in the last three months alone that were unnecessarily dragged out because neither party would directly address the issues with integrity and class. Rebecca stopped me after a talk and asked what she should do about her boyfriend who broke up with her four months earlier. Confused, I asked her to clarify. She said that they weren't officially seeing each other any longer, but that they continued to get together a couple times a week and share some intimate moments. I almost drew blood I was biting down so hard on my hand. The relationship was clearly dead, but she was still emotionally involved and limping along. She couldn't go back because there was nowhere to go, but she couldn't move forward because she was still holding on.

So no, you can't continue to be good friends with your ex-boyfriend or girlfriend. When you both get thrown from the horse, get up and walk in opposite directions. You need a clean break so that you can see things clearly again. You are going to want to call each other, send each other sweet e-mails, and just check in on one another because "you care," but these types of activities simply keep the wounds open. I know that you want to believe that you can be good buddies—I want to believe it too—but if you were in a serious and passionate relationship, it can't happen. Every little thoughtful thing you do causes those intimate thoughts to bubble back up to the surface. You need to create *time* and *space* between the two of you in order for God to do His work. Whether or not the two of you can be moderate friends in the future will depend on a myriad of factors, mainly how God heals your hearts.

If you want to be able to walk away from a relationship with a clean conscience, try to do everything you can to remedy your problems before shooting the horse. But when you know the relationship is doomed, make it a quick and painless death.

When you and your partner are on the ground, stunned by the fall and delirious from the failed romantic ride, you still have one more duty to perform. Regardless of whether you were the dumper or the dumpee, you need to ask for forgiveness for all your shortcomings once you are emotionally stable and feel that you can speak without pointing the finger or placing blame. It will be a humbling process, but if you can be specific about where you could have done better, you will not only set yourself free, but you will free your partner as well. And that was the point of shooting the horse in the first place.

3. Thou shalt walk back to the castle.

Some people suggest that when you get out of a relationship, you just need to get back on a horse and start dating again. You don't. You need to start walking. You need to walk back to the castle and start the entire process over again from square one.

This concept may seem elementary, but it is a big reason why many of us continue to have failed relationship after failed relationship. When you are galloping off into the distance and you have to kill the horse you are riding, you will inevitably be thrown from the steed. This is going to cause excruciating pain. You need time to heal your bleeding heart and let the tears dry. It will certainly seem more convenient to ask another prince who is grazing his horse in the pasture for a ride—it will *feel* easier—but you need to take the time to walk back to the castle. It is on the walk back that you can talk to God, reflect upon the failed relationship, heal your wounds, and pray about the future.

When you are too quick to jump back on another horse, you are more likely to carry your problems and feelings over from the previous relationship. Couples who have been dating for a significant amount of time share intimate moments and feelings. Even when a relationship ends suddenly, the feelings don't. If you hop into another relationship, you are more likely to pick up at the same level of physical and emotional intimacy that you were sharing at the end of your previous relationship. This is not healthy, for you or the person with whom you start the new relationship. And it is a self-destructive cycle that can repeat itself over and over again.

Valerie had this problem. After one of my speeches, this thirty-three-year-old NYC gal approached me, eyes bright but misty. Strikingly beautiful and well-educated, this sweet woman told me that she had basically had one boyfriend after another since she was eighteen. When one didn't work out, she quickly jumped into another relationship to escape the pain and to ignore her feelings. She was like a frog, jumping from lily pad to lily pad looking for the best place to land, never taking a breath in between. But with every jump, things just got worse. She explained that she had become very physically intimate with one man with whom she had a year-and-a-half-long relationship, only to pick up at the same spot physically with her next boyfriend within a couple weeks. It was tearing her apart.

And it *will* tear you apart. But you aren't the only one it will tear apart. On the flip side, one of the most deceptive and painful things you can experience in relationships is when a person leaves you only to immediately date someone else. This is called "switching horses" and it is detestable. While riding off in the distance, some people develop the habit of looking around at the other horses instead of focusing on where their relationship is going. Of course, the other horses always seem to be faster and prettier—and the grass is always greener on the other side. So, in one move, some people jump from one relationship to another, wrecking two sets of relationships at the same time and leaving one rider all alone.

The reason switching horses is so destructive is because in order to coordinate this difficult move mid-gallop, a person has to build an emotional bond with the rider of a different horse while still riding with her prince. This means that the deceiver was not fully engaged in the relationship she was in—she was simply using one person until someone better came along. You cannot possibly determine if the relationship you are in is "the one" if you continue to compare it to all the relationships around you.

If you decide that the relationship you are engaged in is not the right one, it is critical to shoot the horse and walk back to the castle before starting the process all over again. Both the prince and the princess need time to reflect and to figure out what should change in the next relationship. The princess needs to walk back to the castle and prepare to be fought for again. Likewise, the prince needs to walk back to the castle, grab another horse, and find another princess worth fighting for. It is his training. When both parties don't walk back to the castle, they circumvent the processes necessary to cultivate a lasting relationship.

So, how long should you wait until you start dating again? However long it takes for you to walk back to the castle. The longer your previous relationship lasted, the farther the horse galloped away from the castle, the longer it will take you to walk back. After we kill the horse, some of us are going to lie half-dead on the battlefield for a while before we feel healthy enough to get up and walk again. It is different for each of us and will depend on our personalities, dating history, and faith. But the key is to make the crawl, limp, or walk back. You must get back to the castle.

I think many of us skip the walk back because we are more afraid of being alone than of being with the wrong person. It is a self-esteem issue. And it is a trusting-God issue. Some of us don't really trust that God has our best interests in mind, therefore, we feel the need to take matters into our own hands. If God didn't hesitate to sacrifice His own Son so that we could have chance after chance to know Him, He won't hesitate to give you another chance at real, unconditional love. Walk back.

A Broken, Stronger Heart

If you don't learn anything else from this chapter, remember this—once you truly love someone, you *always* love someone. You can't simply "fall out of love" as many claim to do. Real, godly, unconditional love doesn't work like that. It isn't a light switch that can be flipped on and off, and it isn't circumstantial. God doesn't stop loving us at any point for our constant unfaithfulness. He can't because it goes against His very nature—He *is* Love. If somebody tells you that he doesn't love you anymore, he either never really loved you with a sacrificial passion, or he just has an immature way of dealing with the truth that a piece of his heart will be forever yours. Real, Christ-like love is irreversible.

Sometimes couples honestly love one another but ultimately break up. This is the part that makes failed relationships so difficult and walking back to the castle so important. When you break up with someone you truly love, you need to learn how to replace your *close love* with a *distant love.* Take a love that was protecting, comforting, and intimate, and transform it into a love that is prayerful, faithful, and trusting. Your love has to change. Even though it's against your very nature, learn to want the best for your partner, even if the best isn't you. In this way, your ability to love will become *stronger.*

A tree that withstands the pounding of vicious winds and

rains—even to the point of near collapse—becomes more firmly rooted than a tree that is protected by a surrounding forest. The same can be said about the human condition. Those hearts that endure the harshest stress and strain often become the most firmly rooted. The strongest character and the deepest compassion take root through the greatest conflict.

·   ·   ·

This is why dating is so important. Because it is often through the process of breaking up that our hearts expand and our ability to love becomes stronger. If you are able to forgive the very person who has caused you the most pain, then you begin to understand the power of unconditional love. In a sense, you become more like the Savior, and you are able to live and love more abundantly in the next relationship. If you can't forgive, then you become bitter and angry not only with the opposite sex but also with God. Unfortunately, there are many bitter young adults who have yet to forgive those who have hurt them, and so they can't move on. Many of us are prisoners of cells we've built for ourselves.

Believe me when I tell you that I know how hard it can be. There will be memories and déjà vu moments that send your heart racing again—when you see a black Chevy Envoy like the one she used to drive, when you hear his favorite Coldplay song on the radio, when you eat at that Italian restaurant where you had your first date. No matter how many times you break up, it will always feel like a kick to the chest—you will fight and gasp for each breath afterwards. The hardest thing for our hearts to grasp is that when we break up, we lose our dance instructor, our workout partner, our late-night phone caller, our movie date, our fashion consultant, and our best friend. But not our hope. Our hope lies in Christ alone. God always uses our broken relationships to point us to "the one" He has prepared for us in advance.

The burden of a broken heart may make you feel like you've been thrown from a galloping steed. In reality, it is simply the jolt necessary to dislodge all the heartache you've been carrying with you and open your eyes to real, eternal love.

6

When Men Are Passive . . .

Where Are All the Godly Leaders?

"Man was made at the end of the week's work, when God was tired."

MARK TWAIN

Godly men are like the elusive jack-a-lope. There are rumors of them everywhere, but nobody has actually seen one.

As a young man preparing for his future wife, I am horrified to see how so many men handle their personal relationships. Most of the problems that currently exist in the dating world are a symptom of one thing—a lack of true, authentic, Christian male leadership. (Ladies, try to hold the cheering down. . . . We'll get to you in a moment. . . .) Men have not accepted and shouldered their responsibilities as servant-leaders and tender warriors. This has had a devastating effect in the dating world and has misconstrued a number of issues, including how to date and how to maintain healthy sexual boundaries. Women are looking for kings and we're showing up as clowns.

But men aren't entirely to blame for the confusion. Our domesticated Christian culture has misconstrued the image of a godly man. Many churches in America today preach a very feminine gospel, characterized by messages of comfort, compassion, and stability.[1] Jesus certainly exemplified all these characteristics, but first and foremost, He was a man's man. The earthly son of a carpenter and the heavenly Son of God, He was a model of power and heroic sacrifice. He took risks. He enacted change. He challenged authority. He was, without a doubt, a genuine leader. Men wanted to be like Him, and women wanted to be with Him.

But in order to fit into a lot of churches today, a man has to be a khaki-wearing, Starbucks-drinking, minivan-driving, Bible-toting gentleman. He can't be powerful—he has to be polite. And what testosterone-driven man strives to be polite?! The spirit of power that God has instilled in men has been lost amidst floral arrangements and choir practices. We have become civilized, and through our gradual deterioration, men have become passive and lost our desire to lead.

Many who *do* want to lead have abandoned the church, scared of losing their masculinity. They concentrate their efforts on being leaders in other areas of life such as the office, the gym, and the bar. But without a servant's heart, men become leaders for their own benefit, shepherds who feed only themselves. We no longer have Gideons—men who defy the odds and risk their lives for a higher cause.[2] We have corporate executives—men who defy integrity and risk their character for a higher dollar. We no longer have Joshuas—men who don't take no for an answer and march into the Promised

Land.[3] We have professional athletes—men who don't take no for an answer and march into the promiscuous land. We no longer have Davids—men who speak of the Lord's greatness and raise their children.[4] We have absent fathers—men who speak of their own greatness and neglect their children. We have a distorted view of authentic leadership, and it has wreaked havoc on our personal relationships.

Over sixty percent of adults in the sanctuary on Sunday morning are women,[5] and if you ask any one of them what they most desire of a man, they will inevitably say, "I want a leader." But because the culture is so void of them and the church is not training them, we are in very short supply. We know that men have the ability to lead their families in a godly manner, but like the bathroom on the Starship Enterprise, no one ever gets to see it.

To add insult to injury, the feminist movement has been very adamant about equal rights. And to be honest, I couldn't agree with them more. God considers men and women equal, so we should consider them that way too, and grant them equal rights. But just because we are *equal* doesn't mean we are the *same*. There is a monumental difference between *equality* and *sameness*. Men and women should have equal rights to things such as voting and compensation, but when it comes to how we think and act, we are completely, naturally, thoroughly, one hundred percent different. Not one better than the other, just different, both reflecting unique qualities of the same God. When we embrace our differences, we get a much deeper and broader view of this miraculous thing called life.

Please don't misunderstand me: I'm not suggesting that women can't be leaders. In fact, some women impact the world far more effectively than men do. Oprah, Mother Teresa, and Princess Diana are just a few names that come to mind. But God specifically designed men to lead and serve their wives. By doing so, we use the gifts instilled in us and free our wives to do the same.

Countless men have been caught with their pants down in their relationships—both literally and figuratively. We are spectators in the dating battle even though we are called to be soldiers. It is time that we pull our pants back up and clothe ourselves in the full armor of God. There is a battle out there, and the women need us.

Gentlemen, let me assure you that this mission isn't for the faint of heart. If you decide to be a godly leader, men will ridicule you, women will seduce you, the church will disown you, and society will mock you. You'll have to exercise self-discipline, humility, and sacrificial love, and you'll have to be a rebel against the normal way of dating. If you are tired of being passive and lackadaisical, then remember these five phrases. . . . Get Down, Get Up, Get Out, Get Through, and Get Good at Doing Nothing.

Get Down!

You are never taller than when you get down on your knees.

When a man properly proposes to the woman he loves, he kneels down. Have you ever wondered why a man goes down on one knee to ask for a woman's hand in marriage? I mean, why doesn't he just look her in the eyes or toss the ring in her lap and say, "Keep it if you want it!" It is because he loves her. Kneeling down is a sign of respect and submission. He wants her to know that he plans to serve her. With his actions, he is promising to make her a *priority* for the rest of his life. In return, he is asking her to respect his *position*. He submits to battling for her heart, and she submits to letting him lead. It is a mutual submission in love.

Matthew Henry, the English nonconformist minister and Bible commentator, once said, "Woman was taken out of man; not out of his head to top him, nor out of his feet to be trampled underfoot; but out of his side to be equal to him, under his arm to be protected, and near his heart to be loved." But if you mention the word *submission* in most circles, you will be met with a firestorm of fury. It is not because submission is necessarily bad, but rather because men have done such a poor job modeling it. Wives are to submit to their husbands *as their husbands submit to the Lord.*[6] Here is where the problem lies—men are submitting themselves to no one. We, as men, have broken the circle of life by making ourselves the sole power and authority. We have shown no respect for the position or power of God. In other words, we have made life about us and our own personal desires. Would you want to submit yourself to somebody who thought that the world revolved around him? Is it any surprise that women have taken matters into their own hands? They are simply following our selfish example.

Submission is not slavery or bondage. It means to yield or "to set yourself under." Christ submitted to His Father's plan when He willingly gave His life on the cross. In His infinite wisdom, He knew that in order to truly love another, you must be willing to lay down your life for them. Men *pay this grace forward* to their wives by submitting themselves to Christ. It is a bold act of love and sacrifice.

In the movie *Gladiator,* Maximus is the Commander of the Armies of the North and General of the Felix Legions. He is a mighty warrior, highly respected by his men for both his wisdom and experience. Because of his great leadership, he has expanded the Roman kingdom and made it one of the most powerful empires in history. But when the emperor, Marcus Aurelius, asks him to do one more thing before he returns home, Maximus quickly snaps to attention and says, "What will you have me do, Caesar?"

Doesn't it seem odd that Maximus is so eager to obey Caesar's command? After all, Maximus is the greatest fighter in Rome and could easily strike down the aging emperor. He has thousands of soldiers who are loyal to him. He could take the throne by force. He could do whatever he wanted. But instead of exercising his own free will, he decided to obey Caesar and serve Rome. It was an act of humility and strength. By submitting himself to a greater authority, he made himself part of a greater cause.

Although many of us are successful businessmen, athletes, fathers, and boyfriends, we need to submit ourselves to a greater Authority (God) so that we can serve a greater cause

(His Kingdom). The mark of a saint is the ability to refuse your own free will for the good of others. Maximus submitted to Caesar because Caesar held a greater *position*. God holds a greater *position* in our lives and deserves our allegiance. If we are to ask our future wives to submit themselves to us as leaders of our families, then we must exemplify this servant-leadership by asking God, "What will You have me do, Lord?"

Christ modeled this behavior when He knelt down and washed the disciples' feet.[7] He reminded us that in order to lead, we must first serve. I've yet to meet a woman who is upset because her man plans too many romantic dinners, cleans up around the house, opens the door for her, and prays for each meal. Women are happy to yield to their men when their men make decisions out of sacrificial love and service.

Submission doesn't make you weaker—it makes you stronger. When Christ submitted to His Father's plan, He was seated at the right hand of God. When man submits to Christ, he can ask for anything in accordance with His name and it will be given to him. When a woman submits to her godly husband, she will be cherished, adored, protected, and comforted.

But men have to start the cycle by making themselves sub-missive to Christ. God has already done His part, and the women are anxiously waiting for us to do our part. Because it is our responsibility to lead our families, God will hold us accountable for *all* the decisions made in our house. Even though Eve was the first to eat the fruit from the forbidden tree, Adam was held accountable for her actions.[8] God had given Adam the position of authority, but because he didn't make his wife a priority, she was lured into sin.

One of my favorite movie scenes is in *Indiana Jones and the Last Crusade* when Indy (Harrison Ford) is walking down a dangerous corridor in an attempt to find the Holy Grail. As he walks to the entranceway, we see two decapitated men who sought the Grail lying dead in front of him. Slowly shuffling passed the corpses, he begins mumbling to himself, "The Breath of God . . . only the penitent man will pass. Only the penitent man will pass . . . the penitent man . . . the penitent man . . . the penitent . . . the penitent. . . ." As he reaches the spot where both men were killed and he feels a rush of air, Indy explodes out of his mumbling and shouts, ". . . The penitent man is humble before God. . . . He kneels before God. . . . *Kneel!!*" And as he hits his knees, a sharp triple pendulum razor buzzes over his head, just missing his body.

If you want to be a servant leader, you have to learn to lead from your knees. You can't expect to speak with authority in your relationship unless you are under Authority.

Get Up!

Many television commercials suggest that old men are having trouble getting it up. But if you ask me, I think it is the young men that are having trouble getting it up.

The courage, that is. Most young men today just don't have the courage to be godly men and transformational leaders. God has given them all the tools they need for life and holiness, but they simply lack the internal fortitude to make a difference. And that is sad. Some of God's greatest leaders were young men. David was just a shepherd boy when he struck down the mighty Goliath.[9] Daniel was in his twenties when he became one of the chief advisors to the powerful Nebuchadnezzar.[10] Jesus himself started His ministry when He was thirty years old and within three years had changed the world forever.[11] They took God's Word to heart—"Don't let anyone look down on you because you are young, but be an example to believers in speech, in life, in love, *in faith, and in purity*" (emphasis added).[12]

The world is desperate for those types of leaders today, especially with regard to faith and purity. We live in a culture saturated by sex. As you'll soon read in chapter 9, young men desire to have wild, passionate, hot, unbelievable sex. And there is absolutely nothing wrong with that . . . as long as it is within the framework of marriage. God made us physical creatures, and He wants us to enjoy our wives. But most of us have abused our freedom as singles, polluted our own bodies, and stood idly by as others have flaunted their lustful behavior. What's worse is that we have acted as though we have no responsibility for our sexual behavior and that it can't be restrained.

Where are the men who will say, "Do not arouse or awaken love until it so desires"?[13] Who, among today's so-called leaders, will take the initiative in their romantic relationships and honor God with their bodies? It is easy to do what the rest of the dating world is doing. It takes no self-control or self-respect to sleep around. You merely have to be male. But it takes a real man to respect a woman enough not to take advantage of her.

Arguably one of the most successful singles in the history of mankind was a sharp young man by the name of Joseph. When Joseph was in his early thirties, he was second in command in Egypt. Before he attained such prominence, however, he had numerous challenges that tested his character. One of the most notable was a close encounter with his boss Potiphar's wife.[14] Tempting and suggestive, Potiphar's wife had tried to get Joseph to sleep with her on numerous occasions. When none of her manipulative plans worked, she simply grabbed Joseph and began dragging him into bed. Instead of just enjoying a quickie with a powerful woman who could help his career, he fled from the house naked. Joseph did what most men today deem impossible—he resisted casual sex with a beautiful woman.

Let's put things in perspective, gentlemen. God isn't asking us to lift a Volkswagen over our heads or to floss an angry alligator. He isn't asking the impossible. He is asking us to do something He has already empowered us to do—save ourselves for our wives. It is just that most of us are choosing not to do it.

Unfortunately, most of pop culture supports the preconceived notion that a virgin man is about as dangerous as a serial killer. Or he is someone who couldn't get any action even if he wanted to. In the movie *The 40 Year Old Virgin*, Andy Stitzer is portrayed as an anal, introverted electronics superstore clerk, who not only has a full collection of action heroes and comic books at home but also rides his bike to work. Not exactly the type of man most of us aspire to be. But in the Bible, a slightly more reliable source of living information, Joseph is described as "well-built and handsome." And he left an unforgettable legacy behind. Quite a contrast to the nerdy and awkward virgin men Hollywood portrays today, isn't it?

But the Joseph image of a man won't be the norm until men get up the courage to change their ways. Right now, too many men are content being successful, not significant. They are happy being brash, not bold. They are satisfied with letting women decide how far to take things physically in a dating relationship. When was the last time you heard a man say, *"Well, she threw me down on the couch, but before things got too hot and heavy, I told her that we needed to slow down."* How about never?! We make women do that.

There will always be men who see women as objects of pleasure rather than objects of affection. But you don't have to be one of those men.

Get Out!

If you want to have an amazing romance, you have to get out and fight for your lady.

In *Wild at Heart,* John Eldredge says it best: "A man longs for somebody to fight for, and a woman longs to know she is worth fighting for."[15] Part of the problem is that the overly cautious Christian culture has made dating about as adventurous as finger painting. We have sterilized the dating environment by fitting pastors with flame retardant suits and allowing them to extinguish any spark of passion. While the intention was to make sure that couples stay dead from the waist down, the reality is that it has killed most young adults from the waist up. Many Christian men are now about as rugged and dangerous as Rain Man.

Have you ever noticed how women are often attracted to the "bad boy" image? Do you know why? Because bad boys are dangerous and adventurous. They don't set out to be nice. They break rules, ignore traditions, stir up chaos, and live life on the edge. They are rebels who are tough, unbound, and free. In many ways they are like . . . Jesus.

But most Christian men are not adventurous. The only thing we fight is the traffic on the way to our weekly Bible study. We have buried our true hearts, which beat for adventure and discipline. As men, we learn how to become godly husbands by fighting for our ladies during the dating process. We sharpen our leadership skills by mounting the steed, fighting the dragon, and scaling the castle walls. When this training is removed by instituting layers of ridiculous dating rules, we are completely unprepared to be the husbands that our wives need us to be.

Men need to be actively engaged in the dating process not only for their own development, but also to nurture the hearts of their girlfriends. If a woman's heart is a flower, too many of them are wilting right now. Women long to know they are worth fighting for, and they desperately want to be part of the adventure of love. "Do You think I'm beautiful?" is the question that Angela Thomas poses to God in her book by the same title.[16] Women need confirmation that they are lovable and beautiful just as they are. Because so many men show women "love" only through sex, women have doubled their efforts to get our attention by getting breast enhancements, hiking up their skirts, and lowering their morals. We, as passive men, have forced them to find superficial ways to attract our attention. Everything we do and everything we *don't* do has an impact. By focusing on sex and neglecting the deeper issues that resonate in women's hearts, we have caused women to become considerably more desperate.

Sean was an exceptionally articulate young businessman, and when he pulled me aside, I could tell that he was probably a very gifted international consultant. But sometimes our greatest virtues can become our greatest vices. Sean loved his girlfriend of two years, but he was spending more and more time away from her to build his business. When his frustrated girlfriend suggested that they may not have a future together, Sean realized that he had dropped the ball and needed to start pouring into her life again. Because he was often out of town, he had to get creative by sending small gifts, planning surprise getaways, and developing a Bible study they could do together while he was traveling. Slowly, but surely, she began to gain confidence in their relationship again. "My feelings never changed for her," he said with a smile. "I just had to change how I expressed those feelings."

There is no specific formula for getting off the couch and getting back into the battle. It is simply a matter of embracing the power that God has instilled in us as Christian men. There will always be selfish slobs who think that women need to make all the effort. Complaining is a luxury of those who sit on the sidelines of life. Your heart and your woman are awaiting you right on the other side of this ridge. Put on the full armor of God—the belt of truth, the breastplate of righteousness, the feet of readiness, the shield of faith, the helmet of salvation, and the sword of the Spirit[17]—and charge into battle. You already have all the strength and protection you need.

Get Through!

If you want to get through to your woman, you have to speak her language.

Whether you see men and women as clams and crowbars, buffalos and butterflies, or Mars and Venus, one thing is certain—communication is essential to a successful relationship. Even after you have built up the courage to fight for the woman of your dreams, you can't just grab her and throw her over your shoulder like a sack of potatoes. Women are much more delicate than we are, both emotionally and physically, and if you want to win her heart, you are going to have to speak to it.

I know what most men are thinking—*Dang it!* We have become quite comfortable clunking along like a dryer full of army boots. But let me assure you, comrades, that communicating with the opposite sex is not nearly as difficult as we make it out to be. If you know a few basics of successful communication, you will exponentially increase your odds of dating that cover girl you always see around town.

First of all, we need to realize that men and women think differently. Men subscribe to the reflexive theory of thinking while women subscribe to the transitive theory of thinking. In algebra, the *reflexive* property states a=a. In other words, things relate only to themselves. If a man has a problem with a colleague at the office, that has absolutely nothing to do with his dating life. Men compartmentalize their lives and don't allow one area to affect the other. When a man is preparing to go on a date, he runs through a simple checklist of things to do. *Dress nice, check. Bring rose, check. Kiss good night, check.* One action has nothing to do with the other. Men are very project oriented and simple.

Women, on the other hand, subscribe to the *transitive theory* of thinking. The transitive property in math states that if a=b and b=c, then a=c. In other words, everything is interrelated and any action may affect another. So, if a woman has a disagreement with a colleague at the office, she may still be pining over it during her dinner date that night and may need to talk about it before she can really focus on the date at hand.

For the most part, women are very relational and emotional and allow certain actions to affect others. They see the broader picture in life and how we are all connected. When a woman goes on a date, she is very conscious of everything that transpires. If a man dresses nicely, then she may assume he is very excited about the date, a=b. If he also brings a rose, then she may think that this date may become more than just a date, b=c. And if the evening ends with a sensuous kiss, she may presume that this relationship has a future, therefore a=c. Women are constantly making connections in the web of interpersonal relationships.

I don't think I have to explain how this can get both sides into trouble, especially if we are oblivious to how the other side thinks. And neither gender is necessarily right. There is a time to compartmentalize our interactions and there is also a time to embrace our interwoven relationships. In dating, we simply need to be aware that 99.9 percent of the time our partner does not see the same events the same way we do.

In addition to understanding how women think, it is even more important to understand how they communicate what they are thinking and feeling. In *The Five Love Languages,* Gary Chapman suggests that we all speak five emotional languages.[18] The languages are:

> *Words of Affirmation*
> *Quality Time*
> *Receiving Gifts*
> *Acts of Service*
> *Physical Touch*

Every person can speak all five languages, but people usually tend to have one primary language and one secondary language. For example, the primary love language for most women is quality time, meaning that they experience love and romantic feelings when their men give them their undivided attention. This can be expressed by going for a long walk, sitting around and talking, or simply watching television together. Women whose primary love language is quality time just want their men to be around and focused on the relationship.

On the other hand, the primary love language for the majority of men is physical touch. This isn't just sexual contact, although the sexual experience may be part of it. Most men feel loved when their women have their hands, legs, or other parts of their body touching them. While many men may be too macho to grab their lady's hand while they are walking, most men feel like a king when their girl takes the initiative and grabs his arm. Men are physical beings and like to have contact with the women they love.

The five languages are pretty simple and self-explanatory, but they are extraordinarily important. If you don't know which language your girlfriend speaks, you may be talking to her in a language she only vaguely understands. If your girlfriend's primary language is quality time and you constantly encourage her with words of affirmation, she will not feel loved. You can call her every hour on the hour and tell her, "I love you, shoopsie-poo!" but if you aren't ever physically present and attentive, the relationship is doomed.

To make matters worse, because women think transitively, if you don't spend time with a quality time girlfriend, she will think: *Well, if he isn't spending time with me, that must mean he isn't interested. And if he isn't that interested, we have no future together.* If a=b and b=c, then a=c. In your heart, you may know that you've found the woman of your dreams, but if you don't fulfill her needs by speaking her language, she will slip away from you.

Sean, the international consultant I mentioned earlier, started to repair his relationship with his girlfriend by sending her special little gifts from every country he visited. But her primary love language was words of affirmation. It wasn't until Sean developed a Bible study that they could do together over the phone that the relationship started getting better. By encouraging her in a couple's study, he was able to speak to her heart and save his relationship.

Pretty mind-blowing, isn't it? You're probably asking yourself, *Why didn't they teach me* that *in high school instead of geometry?! Those are the angles I needed to learn.* Well, now you know. It's time that we starting getting through to our girlfriends.

Get Good at Doing Nothing!

Men, this point is the easiest to understand and the hardest to implement. You know what most women want and expect from us? Nothing. They just want *us.* All of us. All of our hopes, fears, goals, and thoughts. They want to share in our most precious dreams, and they want to touch the deepest parts of our souls. They want us to be vulnerable, and they want us to be real. They want us to be the leaders and men

God designed us to be. For the most part, they don't want us to take them anywhere or buy them anything (although roses and diamonds help grease the wheels from time to time). Women just want us, and they want our love.

This means that we are going to have to throw out the old dating handbooks that suggest we take them to movies, posh dinners, and crowded dance clubs. This also means that we have to stop solving every problem they pose to us in conversation. News flash, gentlemen—they already know the answer; they are simply sharing the story with us to see if we are listening! We need to get creative at finding ways to express our hearts and personalities in our dates.

One idea that my friend Rhett had was to cook dinner for his girlfriend once a week. He wouldn't tell her what they were having for dinner. She would just show up at his place every Wednesday night and be surprised. Another buddy, Greg, decided that he and his girlfriend were going to read a romance novel together out loud. So, one night he would read to her and the next night she would read to him. But the young man who most impressed me—a gentleman whose name I promised to keep confidential so that his buddies wouldn't roast him—was the one who decided to treat his girl to a manicure and pedicure, which he was going to give to her! After we both laughed for over half an hour, he told me how he went online to figure out how to do it and also had a pedicure himself so that he could see how it was done. This man was serious about pouring his heart into his girlfriend's life!

How we express ourselves will vary because our personalities are unique and our girls are different. We just have to learn how to do nothing. And do it very, very well.

.   .   .

Most of the problems in the dating world stem from the simple fact that men have forgotten how to be men. Instead of focusing on women's hearts, we have focused on their bodies, and this error has had devastating effects throughout our culture. One of the most eye-opening things I've learned about women, even extremely confident women, is that they have insecurities. Whether these insecurities are emotionally or spiritually rooted, we have to be sensitive to them and realize that part of our responsibility is to protect their hearts. Even the strongest women are beautifully fragile.

People often say that communication is the most difficult part of any relationship, but that is not necessarily true. You certainly have to work on speaking to one another's hearts, but no matter how transparent you are, communication will break down from time to time. That is when a man is put to the true test. The defining characteristic of unconditional love is forgiveness. Can you forgive? Will you? Gandhi once said, "Forgiveness is an attribute of the strong. The weak cannot forgive."

It's time for men to be strong again. One thing we can no longer be is passive. Because when men are passive . . .

7

. . . Women Are Desperate

Where Are All the Confident Women?

"When men attempt bold gestures, generally it's considered romantic. When women do it, it's often considered desperate or psychotic."
CARRIE, *SEX AND THE CITY*

My brother has an alarm clock in his room that we all jokingly refer to as Hell's Bells. It is one of those early-twentieth-century alarm clocks that you have to wind up. It is a little oversized, the numbers are almost worn off, and it still has the two original copper bells on top. And to say it is loud is a gross understatement. When it goes off, it sounds like a herd of elephants are racing across a wood floor with metal trash cans duct-taped to their feet. It is just slightly less painful than whacking your shin with a crowbar. I'm surprised his neighbors don't bolt out of their apartments every time it rings thinking the entire complex is on fire. The first time I heard it I thought someone had strapped a tornado siren to my head.

Fortunately, when my brother decides he doesn't want to wake up next to an air horn, he can simply throw the alarm clock away. But most women aren't so fortunate. They have an internal clock ticking that awakens their emotions with a siren louder than Hell's Bells. And they can't turn it off.

Nor should they have to—they were intricately and delicately designed that way. Women desire to be desired. They long to share in an adventure. And there is nothing wrong with this . . . except when a woman's identity is founded in her romantic relationship. Women run into heart-wrenching problems when their desire *to be loved* overrides their desire *to love.*

The Proverbs 31 woman is the standard by which many women measure themselves, and for good reason. The woman described in that chapter of the Bible is godly, loving, disciplined, faithful, and wise. She is an entrepreneur, importer, athlete, manager, realtor, farmer, homemaker, and exceptional wife. Some people imagine a Christian woman barefoot and pregnant, completely subservient and domesticated, but this passage of the Bible shatters that false stereotype. Godly women have strong character, many skills, and great compassion. They aren't just "help mates" as many churches describe them. They are, as the proper translation shows us, "life-savers"—a term used in other parts of Scripture only to denote God.[1] They are equal partners, in marriage and in life, who love their men through situations that they could not conquer alone.

And that is sexy. Very sexy. Our culture has misconstrued the term *sexy* to refer only to a woman's outward appearance—how big her breasts are or how tight her pants fit. But a woman is truly sexy when she reflects the characteristics of a godly woman, when she is confident in her own skin, and when she manifests these qualities in her actions and her appearance. The women who grace the pages of most men's magazines aren't sexy. They are trashy. There is nothing sexy about being more plastic than a Barbie doll and being handled more than a puppy at a petting zoo.

Most godly men desire to battle for a sexy woman. We long to have a woman by our side who "we can have full confidence in, who lacks nothing of value."[2] But a wife of noble character is hard to find. Because so many men haven't accepted their responsibilities as boyfriends, women have altered their roles as girlfriends. There are a number of misconceptions about the role of godly women in today's culture. Let's address a few that have been the most detrimental.

4 Fallacies Surrounding Godly Women

1. Godly women aren't desperate.

We may want to believe that godly women aren't desperate—they certainly don't need to be—but the sad fact is that many of them are. Instead of embracing the season of singleness, some morally convicted women circle like vultures, eyeing the barren plains for the lone godly man to come stumbling across. Heck, some Christian women don't even care if he is a fruit-bearing believer—as long as he goes to church, he is dateable material and free game! Don't believe

me? Go to any university, restaurant, Bible study, or concert
and listen to the conversation. If the discussion veers away
from men, it is only in favor of shopping and chocolate.

I understand that the heart of a woman desires to be pursued, embraced, and fought for. But desperation isn't sexy.
Men can spot a desperate woman a thousand yards away with
a blindfold on. You can't expect a knight to fight for your
heart if you are willing to bail out of the tower without a battle, dear princess. And most women are doing just that by asking men out on dates, lowering their standards, and seducing
them with sexual favors. Fearful of being alone, they position
themselves on the window ledge, prepared to pounce on the
first prince who passes.

Part of the fault for women's desperation lies directly on
the shoulders of us young men who have dated selfishly.
Women have become desperate *because* men have become
passive. We have done a poor job reminding you that you are
beautiful, lovely, exotic, and cherished. But even though we
have neglected you, your inner contentment should not be
based on your romantic relationship. Men do not "complete
you." Your hearts should be set on the Lord and on things
above. Do not be anxious about getting married—have faith
that at just the right time, when both you and he are ready—
the Lord will bring a prince.

One woman shared her revelation with *Today's Christian
Woman*. She said, "I realized a long time ago, before I got married, that to get the caliber of man I wanted, I had to raise my
standards as a woman. I threw myself into God's Word and

learned as much about Him as I could. I found things I enjoyed doing and began doing them. I found out who I was as a person. I not only began to feel better about myself, but I began to feel worthy of love, and worthy of waiting for someone who'd offer me more than just a feel-good in the middle of the night."[3]

I don't think it is a coincidence that one of the most highly rated shows on television right now is *Desperate Housewives*. I think most women feel neglected, both while dating and while married. When women don't get the questions *Am I lovely?* and *Am I beautiful?* answered by the men in their lives, they look elsewhere to fill that need. They get desperate for confirmation that their lives mean something and that they are adored.

But when women get desperate, men get nervous. The other day one of my friends told me that the next guy she dated was going to be "the one." A week earlier, I overheard two late twentysomethings talking about how one of them had been dating this guy for two weeks, and she knew he was "the one." Two weeks! Ladies, you are bringing a lot of undue pressure into a situation when you have these types of expectations. Do you think guys are going to be lining up to take you out if you say the next guy will be "the one"? That is a lot of pressure, and most guys don't want to subject themselves to unrealistic expectations. Men hate to fail, so do yourselves a favor—make it easy and nonthreatening for a man to ask you out.

There is certainly a shortage of genuine and trustworthy

young Christian men out there—I know that, and I am fighting valiantly to reverse the trend. As women, you can help by reminding men what a godly woman looks like. Be confident, compassionate, and most of all, patient. Remember, desperate women aren't sexy.

2. Godly women should wear the pants.

Unfortunately, men are just figurehead leaders in most romances. They may be the one sitting behind the steering wheel, but they are like Hoke from *Driving Miss Daisy*. They are simply taking instructions on where to go. *Yes, Miss Daisy, I be a-drivin'.* . . .

There is evidence of this everywhere. The whipped puppy-dog look of the guy who was dragged to church by his wife. The incessant calling your colleague does at the office to check in with his partner regarding every decision he makes. The shared e-mail account that a couple has so that the wife can oversee all of her husband's activities. Men may *appear* to be leading, but in many cases it is merely a façade the couple puts on to save face in the judgmental Christian community. The woman really steers the relationship and is puppeteering the whole show from behind the scenes.

The reason many women end up leading their marriage relationship is because they were leading their dating relationships. It was a precedent established at the beginning. We've all heard numerous stories where the woman initiated the original introduction, she supported and fueled the dating process, and she even said "I love you" first and started the talk of engagement. The man never had to be proactive. Like a bobblehead doll, the man simply shook his head in whatever direction the woman instructed.

Most women think they are helping their men by showing them how to lead, but they are really just aggravating the problem and making them more passive. You can't explain to a man how to lead anymore than you can explain to him how to cook. The only way he will learn is by rolling up his sleeves and diving into the kitchen. Men learn to lead by leading. It is a process that is refined during dating and sharpened in marriage. If you don't allow them to lead while dating, don't expect them to lead after the honeymoon.

Sherry, a sweet Southern girl I met at a singles conference, asked, "But what if he is unwilling to lead? Somebody has to wear the pants in our relationship." Sherry, you are absolutely right. Somebody does have to wear the pants in your dating relationship. But these God-designed pants were specifically intended for men and won't fit you. They are extra long to challenge a man's spiritual growth and extra wide to humble his burgeoning ego. You know what happens if you try on pants that are way too big for you, don't you? They end up falling down time and time again everywhere you go. You become vulnerable and exposed. The same will be said about your relationship. It will fall time and time again and you will get hurt. If the guy you are dating is unwilling to lead, then you are dating the wrong guy. *All* men are capable of leading— some just choose not to accept the responsibility.

If you haven't noticed, men are not eager to reciprocate

the flip-flopping of roles. Even though women are willing to wear men's pants, men have no interest in wearing women's pants. In other words, women may be willing to take on the responsibilities of men, but not vice versa. So, if a woman wants to lead, protect, and provide, who is going to be compassionate, nurturing, and supportive? This role is going to remain unfilled. Women will drain themselves trying to overcompensate for the absence of true masculinity, and men will become even more distant and unresponsive as they watch life pass them by from the comfort of the living-room couch.

Ladies, if you have to tell your man how to lead, he is not really leading. *You* are leading. You are simply doing it from behind from the scenes. And that is not beneficial for either of you. Because many men have neglected their role as spiritual and emotional leader, it will take an amazing step of faith on your part to trust his initial steps to lead. He may not have the biblical knowledge that you do and he may not know all the right things to say, but he will learn quickly if you lovingly encourage him. Deep down, most men *want* to lead, but they are unsure they have a safe environment in which to try it. If you don't belittle him, berate him, or veto his every decision, you'll be surprised at how quickly he begins to enjoy his responsibilities.

You can't change a man, only God can do that. But you can plant the seed of encouragement, water it, and validate his significant role as leader and protector of your heart. And that is a wonderful first step.

3. Godly women aren't sexy.

Being sexy isn't a sin. In fact, a woman who fears the Lord and displays the fruit of the Spirit is unquestionably, stunningly, wildly, without a doubt the sexiest thing on the planet.

We do women a terrible disservice when we tell them that their beauty is a sin. The church has become so preoccupied with eradicating all physical sins that we are suffocating our women. By withholding our praise and adoration for both their internal and external beauty, we have forced them to cry out, *Am I beautiful? Am I sexy? Am I worthy of love?* The very essence of a woman is her beauty. God formed man but He *fashioned* woman.[4] He intended for her to reflect His beauty and intrigue. When you tell the woman you love that she is sexy, you get a front-row seat at watching her walk on clouds. With a few simple words, you free her from her insecurities and doubts.

If physical beauty is a sin, then why did God create sunsets, flowers, and babies? Why did He give us the capacity to decipher between the aesthetically pleasing and the degenerate? Why did He make us physical beings at all if He did not want us to enjoy it? I think it is clear that God *does* want us to enjoy the beauty of a woman and our physical nature. But He wants us to keep it in perspective. "For physical training is of *some* value, but godliness has value for *all* things, holding promise for both the present life and the life to come."[5] Our physical condition should never supersede our spiritual one.

The problem is that a lot of church ladies aren't exactly

what you call "sexy." They often have more fabric wrapped around them on a Sunday morning than a circus tent. What's even more disappointing is that there is no joy in their hearts. They have denied the very things that make them a woman of God, and it has left them empty and lost. You want to know why many young women don't want to devote their lives to the Lord? It is because we have told them that they have to deny their hearts—the way the Lord created them—to accept the Lord. We have told them their beauty is in vain.

When women feel sexy, their hearts overflow with passion, and they are freed to pour into other people's lives. The sexiest women are often the most nurturing and compassionate because they are confident in who they are. The reason women enjoy shopping more than men is because it is a natural extension of their original design. They long to be pretty. Women are often also the best interior designers because they have a sense for what looks good. Most men don't even know that "tangerine" and "camel" are colors!

There is an unspoken rule in many Christian circles that women should deny their physical beauty. The thinking goes: The more covered you are, the more humble you are. And the more humble you are, the holier you are. If a woman embraces her beauty, she is often gossiped about by the other women of the church and reprimanded by the male leaders. I find it interesting that when the adulterous woman was brought before Jesus, He didn't say, "For heaven's sake, woman, cover your body! No wonder you got yourself into this!" Instead He just said, "Go and sin no more."[6]

Jesus knew that her physical beauty was not the issue—it was simply a symptom of an uncommitted heart. Women who feel like they need to flaunt their breasts and bottoms do so because they don't feel beautiful inside. And this is where the real danger lies. When women try to fill their internal emptiness with their external appearance, things spiral out of control. You can never be physically sexy enough to fill a gap where the Lord's love has to reside. But physical beauty, in and of itself, is not a sin.

There is a group of Christian girls in my community whom I really admire. Some are tall, some are short, some are skinny, some are fat, some are black, and some are white, but together they've learned how to embrace their diverse beauty. And they have a saying that I just love—*Don't short the sexy!* From my limited male understanding, it means, "Don't deny the beauty that God placed inside you, for when you do, you deny the fact that you are a woman." They know that they are not all supermodels, but it doesn't stop them from being fashionable and sexy. They aren't flaunting their goods nor are they being indecent. They simply believe that you should be the same gorgeous woman inside the church as you are when you are outside. It is no wonder that no one in this group of single ladies is ever without a date. They have embraced their femininity.

Women like Pamela Anderson, Carmen Electra, and Anna Nicole Smith are not sexy. They are empty—and they are trying to mask that emptiness with physical beauty. *Sexy* is a term reserved for those women who accept the beauty that God has given them and reflect it in every aspect of their life, including the physical.

Don't short the sexy! Don't suppress the splendor and magnificence that is woman. Go ahead and flaunt it.

4. Godly women aren't seductive.

I'm going to let you in on a little secret. One of a man's greatest fears is that the woman he marries will play the same trick as his dog . . . she will roll over and play dead in bed. No man wants to marry a Victorian-minded woman who believes she should only have sex out of duty to her husband. *Do it for the Queen and for England!* is not exactly the erotic talk a man hopes to hear on his wedding night.

Why do you think so many guys believe it is necessary to have sex before getting married? They fear that they may marry a "nice Christian girl" who suppresses her sexual desires and is about as hot and passionate as a block of ice. Men want some indication that the woman they are marrying is passionate.

But at the heart of the issue, it isn't even about sex. It is about *mystery* and *intrigue*. It is about *passion* and *romance*. Men want their lives to be full of adventure and a little unpredictable. We don't want somebody who is just warm, nice, and polite. If we wanted someone like that, we would buy a dog! We would rather date a woman who attacks life like a cage fight, a free spirit that follows the Lord with reckless abandon. Some men marry for safety, but a man after God's own heart will marry a woman who challenges him. Many of us single gentlemen would be more willing to take a blind date with a woman who came with an explicit warning: *She's kind of a loose cannon. She's going straight to heaven or straight to hell, but either way, she's taking the bullet train!*

Not coincidentally, godly women have been perfectly equipped to fill this kind of role. But very rarely do you see it among Christian women today. If you were to glance at the women in churches across the nation, you might assume that a Proverbs 31 woman is defined by someone who is prim, proper, and dignified at all times. (You may also assume that the answer to every question is "I'm blessed" and that you are not a real Christian if you don't have your name inscribed on your Bible.) But if you were to read through the Bible, you would find that the women God chose to use were scandalous, passionate, faithful, vulnerable, and seductive. Simply stated, they were women not afraid to be women. Mary, Jesus' mother, got pregnant out of wedlock.[7] Rahab, the Gentile prostitute in Jericho, committed treason by harboring the spies from Moses' camp.[8] Mary Magdalene, the misunderstood follower of Christ who was present at both the crucifixion and resurrection, had seven demons driven out of her.[9] And then there is Ruth.[10]

If you have been to any women's Bible study in America, you have probably studied Ruth. She is the poster girl for finding a godly man. With the help of her mother-in-law, Naomi, Ruth went from being a widow to being the wife of Boaz, a good and honorable man. But this transition happened in a most unforgettable way, a method completely unacceptable in most churches today: Ruth seduced Boaz.[11]

It wasn't one of those pay-per-view seductions that you watch on Direct TV or some shallow, lustful fling because her hormones were raging. In fact, it had nothing to do with sex. She enticed him with her pure heart. She attracted him by being of noble character. She seduced him with godly integrity.

Boaz first recognized Ruth while she was working in his field. He immediately took interest in her and showed her favor by protecting her. When Ruth told Naomi how kind Boaz had been, Naomi immediately put the ball in play. Naomi was a godly woman in her own right, and being older and wiser, knew what it took to get a man. She told Ruth, "Wash and perfume yourself, and put on your best clothes." Basically, "Get ready, Cinderella, you're going to the ball!" She then instructed Ruth to be very discreet, go to the evening dinner, and wait until Boaz was alone and sleeping before approaching him.

That evening, Boaz had far too much fun with the boys and ended up getting drunk. Instead of going home, he ended up passing out "at the far end of the grain pile." Looking all foxy and cute, Ruth approached Boaz quietly and unnoticed by anyone else. At this point, she had two options: She could either (1) take advantage of the inebriated Boaz, have sex with him, and then demand that he fulfill the Israelite custom by marrying her, or (2) take the road less traveled, be a woman of noble character, and sleep quietly at his feet until morning. She chose the latter and fell asleep at his feet.

When Boaz awoke in the middle of the night and realized all that Ruth had done to protect his identity and reputation, he was overwhelmed with gratitude and was even more attracted to Ruth than before. Like the text says in Proverbs 31, he "arose and called her blessed." She had proven her character and identity, and this spurred Boaz to be very decisive in his next move. He set out to marry her.

By being provocative and alluring, Ruth was able to win the heart of Boaz. She didn't approach him in the fields with a bunch of the other girls. She didn't tempt him with her nakedness as he slept. She put on her favorite strapless dress that she wore only on special occasions, sprayed herself with some love potion from Victoria's Secret, and slipped mysteriously into the night. Her presence wasn't inappropriate. It was *intriguing* and *inviting*. She didn't give herself over to Boaz—she just showed him how lucky he would be if he had her!

Now, I know that many women's groups are not going to support the idea that Ruth seduced Boaz. But she did. Maybe if we embraced the fact that godly women can be seductive and sexy, there wouldn't be so many confused singles and unsatisfied couples. When women are free to be the women God created them to be—beautiful, mysterious, and passionate—men step up to the plate and become strong, powerful, and decisive.

Did Ruth take a risk by approaching Boaz? Absolutely. But faith is a step out into the unknown. You can't expect to experience a love that makes you soar like an eagle if your feet never leave the ground. So if you truly desire a good and honorable man, you may want to try a different approach instead of flirting at bars and waiting at churches.

You may want to try being intriguing, mysterious . . . seductive . . .

.   .   .

Carrie Bradshaw, the main character from *Sex and the City*, said something rather profound in one of the episodes. She said, "Maybe some women aren't meant to be tamed. Maybe they're supposed to run wild until they find someone—just as wild—to run with."

It's true. Some women—godly women—are meant to run wild. You should never corral something as beautiful and natural as the female heart. When you try, you cripple a woman's passion for life and limit her blossoming beauty. God didn't make women raw and carnal—He made them delicate and precious. He made them compassionate and nurturing. He made them sexy and seductive. When we embrace the qualities that were uniquely crafted for a woman, we get to see her shine. And when she shines, her light reveals a hidden side of God that we would not have seen otherwise.

8

"Meating" People
How to Meet Quality People
without Becoming a Twelve-Ounce Treat

*"Behold the turtle. He makes progress only
when he sticks his neck out."*
JAMES BRYANT CONANT

The big question for a lot of singles is, "How do I meet quality people without feeling like I'm at a meat market?" At most singles events, you get a name tag and a twelve-ounce T-bone wrapped around your neck as soon as you walk in the door. These groups often have a tendency to draw crowds of people who are solely interested in finding their significant other. Although the planners try to wrap the evening around some type of activity, concert, movie, etc., every cowboy there knows why he moseyed in the door—to partner up!

Many singles have been encouraged to look for a possible mate at church, at a Bible study, or at some other Sunday-morning event. I've received thousands of e-mails from people saying that they just can't find Mr. or Mrs. Bear-My-Children at their home church. You know why? *Because church services and Bible studies are not designed to be matchmaking services.* While it is possible to meet the person of your dreams during Communion, that is not its original intent. Our church services are designed to cultivate a deeper relationship with Jesus Christ, a place for believers to encourage one another, and a sanctuary from the troubles of everyday life. They are not designed to help you find a Friday-night movie date.

We put an unfair burden on the church when we expect it to fulfill the romantic holes in our lives. Things should be measured by the standard for which they were created. Church was designed to nurture and build a relationship with Christ, not to provide a platform for singles to find their spouse. Many churches have done a great job serving their burgeoning singles population by creating fun events and outings, but this should always remain secondary to their primary purpose: to share the light of Christ.

I'm not suggesting that you close your eyes to the possibility that you may meet some intriguing young stud at church. I'm just reminding all of us, myself included, that we shouldn't *expect* the church to play a role for which it is not equipped. The shared responsibility for finding a marriage partner is between you and God, not you and the church. God may use the church, but He also may use a number of other avenues. Unpredictable and mysterious, God is notorious for bringing people together in miraculous ways.

We often hear stories from well-meaning pastors and church leaders about how they met their spouse at church, but this isn't how it normally works. You have to remember, pastors spend the majority of their time at church; we don't. In fact, most of the couples whom I admire have crazy stories about how they bumped into their dream partner. One very energetic elderly couple, Larry and Susan, met at dinner one night. He was eating alone while on a business trip, and she was waitressing his table. They struck up a conversation, and he decided to wait until she got off work to finish it. That was forty years ago. Robert and Rachael met while he was in the hospital, healing from a motorcycle accident. She was his nurse. My own parents met when Mom and the girls were going to Dairy Queen, and Dad and the boys were going to the bar. Dad "happened" to box my Mom's car in and told her he wouldn't move it until she talked to him for a bit. I guess you know the rest.

Part of the problem is that many of us have preconceived notions about what our romance should look like. I can't tell you how many times I've heard a narrow-minded Christian say, "I don't want to meet my husband in a bar," or "Internet dating is for desperate people," or "Church is the only place to find good, godly people." O ye of little faith! When Jesus walked among them, I'm sure the people doubted, "He'll never feed all five thousand of us with five loaves and two fish,"[1] or "I'll give you five-to-one odds Lazarus doesn't come out of the tomb,"[2] or "He is only going to embarrass Himself when that blind man still can't see."[3] But our God defies expectations, leaps over stigmas, and makes the impossible, possible. Do you want to write your love story or do you want God to? If you would like Him to, then put down the pen and slowly back away from your expectations. Deep down, you don't really know the type of person you should marry.

The reason that Christ told us to "go and make disciples of the nations" was that He knew our proclivity to resist change and to lean on our own understanding. If He hadn't told the early disciples to "go," they would have sat around and discussed the power of God among themselves, keeping the miracle of eternal love in a small, tight-knit group. Kind of like we do today in many instances. By our actions, we often tell God that we don't think His love can work in pool halls, sporting events, corporations, Mary Kay parties, restaurants, tractor pulls, and Harley rallies. We limit the locations and venues where God's love can shine through us because we simply won't "go."

Even as I write this, I can sense a segment of the single Christian community pushing away from the table. *I don't think I'm open to finding love just anywhere,* you are thinking. *I think I'll just stick to waiting on God.* There is a time and place to wait on God. Like we talked about in chapter 2, you have to stay put to hear God's call for your life and to understand that you are complete in His love alone. But—and I want to stress this or you may miss it—once you hear God's voice, you have to "go." Faith is not waiting for God to do all the work. Faith is stepping out into the unknown, believing that God will act at just the right time. It is understanding that in nearly every situation, there is something for God to do *and* something for us to do.

Does this mean that we, as Christians, should just blindly

participate in all the party scenes and, as the old adage suggests, "when in Rome, do as the Romans do"? Far from it. Just realize that you don't have to drink to go to a bar. You don't have to dance explicitly to go to a concert. You don't have to curse and act unruly to chill at a basketball game. The light of Christ shines in every situation, and it appears even brighter when surrounded by darkness and confusion. A single light in a room full of lights will not attract much attention, but a single light in a room full of darkness is truly something special. It will attract people of all kinds, both those who need the Light and those who share the Light. The challenge for Christ-followers is to be able to tell the difference.

I hate to point out the obvious, but that lump three feet above your rear end is your brain. God gave it to us for a reason. He wants us to *use* it. We are called to love the Lord our God not only with all of our heart, soul, and strength, but also with our minds.[4] Our social lives should not be constrained to church services and Bible studies, nor should they be limited to bars and concerts. There should be a balance. There are a myriad of other places, possibilities, and people in between, and we need to start exploring these options as well. There are book clubs, charity events, political fund-raisers, university lecture series, art galleries, softball leagues, soup kitchens, and indoor rock-climbing groups. If those don't tickle your fancy, there are Internet services, corporate events, holiday parties, singles conferences, weddings, and speed-dating events. So before you start complaining that "you can't meet any quality people," make sure you have exhausted all the possibilities.

It is no surprise that many of us are still single. We see the same people day after day and never change up our routines. Matt, a handsome and well-educated mid-twentysomething from Arizona, told me that he had trouble meeting new people. He said that he had been going to the same small church since he was a child, he went to work every day with the same team of sixteen people, and his weeknight activities consisted of a Bible study on Tuesday, a church inter-league basketball game on Wednesday, and guys' night on Thursday. I asked him what he was doing to mix it up. He stared blankly at me as if I had just asked him to wrestle a porcupine. Apparently, he thought it was God's job to mix it up for him.

Many of us share this same flawed philosophy, and we remain prisoners of our own habits and routines. When asked about relationships, Warren Buffet wisely noted, "The chains of habit are too light to be felt until they are too heavy to be broken. The chains you put around yourself now have enormous consequences as you go through life." Some of us have put our lives on pause, waiting for the right person to capture our heart before we start hang-gliding, piano playing, swing dancing, and doing all those things we have always dreamed about. But when we approach life this way, we create a two-fold problem because (1) we can't just flip a switch and start living on purpose once Mr. Perfect arrives if we've never done it before, and (2) much of the passion that we experience from doing the things we love is what actually attracts other people to us. It is part of our inner light.

The key to meeting quality people lies in understanding

and living out our passions. Once you have established solid
Godly Characteristics in your life, embrace your Personal
Qualities. These passions will help point you to groups of
people who share common interests. In other words, they will
increase your odds of finding someone with whom you are
compatible.

The Door Called Passion

Although I've never examined Starbucks's financial state-
ments, I'm confident that unmarried Christians have single-
handedly kept the coffee franchise in business. Anytime you
ask a young man or woman where they go to hang with their
friends or where they are most likely to go on a first date
(a.k.a., where they go to discuss "ministry opportunities"),
the answer is Starbucks. While I understand that they make a
killer white chocolate mocha, I'm confused as to why this has
become our sole meeting point. I know that we are not all that
passionate about coffee, no matter how much caffeine and
sugar they inject into it.

But it is convenient. And safe. Like church, we assume that
Starbucks is a good place to meet other quality people who
share our same values. We know that our first priority should
be to find someone who displays the fruit of the Spirit, or
Godly Characteristics. But what we have failed to recognize is
that our Godly Characteristics often shine *through* our Personal Qualities. Our passion for Christ shines through our
activities. If somebody tells you he is a Christian, you have

heard only half of the story. You will get to see if the tree bears any fruit when he plays a game of pick-up basketball or when he takes you to dinner. Was he competitive, yet fair and just, on the basketball court? Was he gentlemanly and courteous at dinner while sympathetic with the overworked waitress? The real question that needs to be answered is: Is his faith evident in what he does?

This is why finding a significant other at church or a Bible study is not always the best option. It is easy to be a Christian around other Christians. A person doesn't need any deep level of conviction to blend into his surroundings there. The real test comes when you leave the protection of the sanctuary and are bombarded by the challenges of daily life. If the guy you are dating can live out his beliefs Monday through Saturday in the money-driven corporate world or in the sex-saturated fashion industry, then you may have a keeper. As James, Jesus' brother, suggested, "Let them show you their faith by what they do."[5]

If you think about it, our Personal Qualities paint a picture of what we are passionate about, and our passion is always linked to a source, whether it is God or our own self-interest. So, when you follow your passion to write music or cater meals, your actions often reveal why you are doing it. Some people do it for simple reasons of self-improvement, but believers do it because it is part of their service to the Kingdom. They are simply exercising their gifts for a greater good.

The reason you need to follow your passions is because you want to marry a person with passion. He may not be passionate about the same things that you are passionate about—in fact, in many marriages, each has very different interests—but he should be rooted in the same source, Jesus Christ. When you are doing those things that make you feel fully alive, you attract and inspire other people to become fully alive. Passion is contagious. And our passion always reveals our source.

So, when you are looking for new environments to meet quality people, engage in those activities that get you excited about life. If you love to cook, serve in a soup kitchen, start a catering business, or throw dinner parties at your house. If you love to golf, join a new country club or teach putting lessons to other adults. If you love to read, enroll in an online community or join a local book club. The opportunities are virtually limitless once we understand ourselves well enough to pursue those things that put a smile on our face.

You may be surrounded by opportunities, but don't just randomly select activities where you think you could meet great people. Horseback riding on Tuesday nights may be an adventure, but not the kind you are going to enjoy if you dislike the outdoors. Do those things that you honestly enjoy doing, and if you don't meet anyone worth dating, at least you will have expanded your horizon and had a good time.

Brett, a guitar player at one of the events where I was speaking, approached me and told me about how he met his wife. He had been a basketball player all his life, but two years into his college career, he tore up his knee in a game. Knowing that his athletic career was finished, he began exploring other pursuits and passions. He had always loved music and decided he wanted to learn to play the guitar. He spoke to a few friends and they suggested that he take lessons with a guy across town. Six months into his lessons, his new teacher suggested that he go to a country bar on new talent night and listen to some of the bands. When Brett walked into the bar, he said he heard "a heavenly voice." Turning the corner, he saw a sweet girl named Amanda singing a song and tickling the strings. He said he couldn't take his eyes off her all night. And from what I understand, he hasn't taken them off her since.

Brett's passion was music. So was Amanda's. But if Brett had ignored his instinct to learn the guitar, he would have missed the road that led him to his wife. When he saw her onstage, Brett didn't know whether or not Amanda was a Christian. But he did know that she loved music, and that shared interest opened a door for conversation. It was through their conversation that Brett saw her strong heart for the Lord. When we embrace our passions, we open doors for new people to enter our lives. Brett's story also has another element that is extremely important—time. Brett had been taking guitar lessons for over six months before he met anyone new and interesting. Don't expect to meet the love of your life at your first ceramics class or in the first month of karate. Be patient and give it time.

Samantha decided to meet new people and expand her group of friends by joining a young professionals group. She decided to join the organization to network with other marketing people in Chicago. After attending mixers and functions for about a year, she was invited to dinner with her new group of friends. As fate would have it, one of the other girls had invited her brother to join them as well. Her very handsome, very single brother! He sat down next to Samantha at the table and they struck up a conversation. When everyone else got up to leave, he invited her to stay for dessert. Of course, she did. He ended up taking her home around midnight that evening, and they've been dating for almost two years now.

I can't tell you what your interests are, but I know that you have them. God places something on all of our hearts. These passions are the road signs you need to follow if you want your life to have meaning and purpose. Some of us travel only a short distance before picking up a life partner, but some of us have longer and more treacherous roads to follow before getting hitched. If you get frustrated on the journey, just remember one thing—the roughest road is the one that leads straight to the top.

Waving Down a Man

It's one thing to talk about the perfect scenario—*boy likes girl, girl likes boy, boy asks girl out on date, girl accepts, boy and girl date and fall madly in love*—but what happens if the man doesn't initiate a relationship? Many Christian men are simply not asking women out in traditional ways, and this dating vacuum is sucking some women down a desperate hole. One of the questions I'm most often asked by women is, "If we shouldn't ask men out on dates, how do we get them to ask us?" It's relatively simple—if you want a man to fight for your heart, give him *permission* to fight for your heart.

I like to refer to it as "the wave." If you are sitting in your castle and notice a dashing young prince, the best way to get the potential suitor's attention is to "wave" at him. This is his sign that you are interested. Most women go to dinner with a group of friends. No matter how confident a man is, most men will not approach a woman who is surrounded by her three best guard dogs. It is just too risky. So, if you want him to come talk to you, catch his eye. Smile at him. Wink at him. Wave at him. Get up and go to the restroom at the same time he does. Send a surprise dessert to his table. Do *something* so that he knows it is safe to introduce himself.

And this advice is biblical. In the Song of Solomon, the beauty asks Solomon, "Where do you tend your sheep?"[6] Properly translated to twenty-first-century lingo, scholars have found that she was asking, "Where is your Starbucks? Where do you hang out so that I can show up there and be noticed by you?" There is a dangerous and erroneous thought circling in some Christian groups that God will miraculously drop the love of your life from heaven, gift-wrapped and marriage-ready. While He certainly can, this appears to be His least used strategy. If you want to be noticed by that dashing hunk across the room, you may have to "wave" at him.

Relationships are a dance—both parties have a role to play. A man may be called to initiate and lead, but the woman has to respond and follow if they are to dance together. Sometimes a man won't ask a woman to dance simply because he doesn't know that she *wants* to dance. As men, we have many skills, but mind reading isn't one of them. Women can help their own cause if they would just position themselves next to the dance floor and let men know they hear "Ol' Blue Eyes" warming up.

Men need only a hint of interest to approach a girl to whom they are attracted. If a woman provides the opportunity, a man will take the initiative. And if he doesn't, then either he isn't interested in her or he is too insecure to risk being rejected. Either way, he is not a good candidate for whom to start painting your nails love-me red.

Elizabeth, a thirtysomething marketing manager, approached me with a stern look on her face after one of my talks. Before she even introduced herself, she blurted out, "I think men should be men and just take the initiative. It shouldn't matter whether we are sending out the vibe or not. They are the ones called to be servant-leaders." Of course, at the time, my first thought was that her body language and approach were exactly what I was talking about. She wasn't being approachable and that was one of the main reasons she was still single. But fearing that she may punch me, I decided to respond a little differently.

Men are called to be servant-leaders, not just servants. And even leaders need cues from the women around them. Ladies, if a man wants to ask you out, he should take the initiative to ask you formally and plan it in advance. But once he starts the volley, it's up to you to hit it back to him. Think of it like a tennis match. He serves—he asks you out to dinner and inquires if there is any type of food you prefer. You hit it back—you either say that you don't care or suggest a restaurant. He volleys again—he tells you that he'll pick you up at seven o'clock. You overhand it back—sounds great. He—talk to you tomorrow. You—wonderful. Bye. Bye. Game point.

But all of this hinges on the fact that you want to play and that you are willing to volley. I've spoken to some Christian women like Elizabeth who think it is solely the man's job to get things moving and keep them moving. One girl said that she wouldn't call a guy for any reason. In fact, she wouldn't even call him *back* if he didn't catch her at home! Another woman said that she wouldn't accept any date unless it was planned out at least three days in advance and the man had to ask her face-to-face.

Has it occurred to anybody that maybe the reason a man doesn't always take the right steps is because he really likes a woman and is scared?! Men have feelings too, and sometimes the thought of asking a beautiful woman out on a date is terrifying. *What if I can't hold an interesting conversation? What about my terrible fashion sense? What if I choose a horrible restaurant?* These are all things that flood our pea brains the very moment we think about asking a woman out to dinner. Cut us a little bit of slack and try to meet us halfway. Any amount of encouragement you can give us would be helpful.

Before you start sending me hate mail disguised as my *Men's Health* subscription, please understand that I'm not advocating that women start asking men out or that women become the leaders in the relationship. I'm simply making a few suggestions that will help you capture a man's attention using your godly figure and not just your womanly figure. Here are a few things to be mindful of when you see that hunka-hunka burning love across the room. . . .

Be noticeable—In most metropolitan cities, a man passes hundreds if not thousands of women during the day. How are you going to make yourself noticeable? What are you going to do so that he introduces himself to you before that blonde who is flaunting her medically enhanced wares a few feet away?

Whether you are at a volunteer function or a corporate party, you have to make some type of concerted effort to be noticed. You are going to have to "wave" at him. Sometimes it will be as simple as standing in his line of sight. Other times you will have to switch the place cards up at the table so that you just "happen" to be sitting next to him. Hopefully, you'll be lucky enough to have a friend who knows him and can introduce you. Regardless of the circumstance, don't be afraid to be noticeable. There is nothing ultra-holy or proper about blending into the crowd. I don't know any godly men who want a woman who is content with just letting life "happen" to her.

One girl "waved" at me recently after I finished playing pool with a couple of my buddies. I noticed this cutie when I first walked into the room but realized she was with two guys and another girl. *A closed door,* I thought. But when I was returning the pool balls, she got in line behind me to rent the table. We struck up a conversation and I found out that she was just hanging out with friends from work. She "waved" at me. I noticed.

The women who are the most noticeable are usually the ones who let their God-given personalities shine through. They don't look like they are trying too hard. They just use what the Lord gave them. In other words, if you are gifted in music and theater, put yourself in situations where your talent comes shining through. If you love sports, go to football and basketball games and express your enthusiasm for the event. As I mentioned earlier, when you pursue your passions, you naturally position yourself to be noticed.

How you dress certainly gets you noticed as well. Men are visual creatures. But we don't notice most of what women think we notice. Very few men are going to compliment you on your Jimmy Choos, your leather Prada bag, or your new pashmina. In fact, most men think a pashmina is a type of African tiger. The many changing fashions and styles are for women to impress one another—rarely do men even notice that your denim jacket is *so* three seasons ago. Men just know what they find attractive and sexy. And less is not always more. Low-riding jeans were made for about five percent of the female population. Unfortunately, the other ninety-five percent is wearing them. Just know that men prefer that you dress to accentuate what you already have, not what fashion says you ought to have.

When my married friends have dinner, they often joke that their wives never know when they are the sexiest. One guy thinks that his wife is most attractive when she is wearing an old sweatshirt and his Yankees cap. A college buddy says jeans and a turtleneck churn his butter. Another friend likes pajama pants and a babydoll T-shirt. Point being, you don't have to flaunt your sexual parts to attract attention. And it won't get you noticed by the right type of guys even if you do.

Be approachable—A woman's body language says much more about her intentions than her words do. Most guys are more likely to engage you and your friend if you are standing shoulder-to-shoulder instead of face-to-face. Just like they taught us in kindergarten, create an open environment that invites others to join your group. If you are standing hands-on-hips or arms crossed on your chest, this is usually the universal sign for "approach-me-and-I'll-rip-your-larynx-out-with-my-curling-iron." Not a real welcoming stance. Try to be relaxed and smile. A sweet smile will take you a long way.

If you are hanging out with a mixed group of men and women, you should be even more conscious of making yourself approachable. You can't expect any man—except the institutionally insane—to approach a group that looks like a bunch of couples. Most of us want to get a phone number, not a black eye. And if a courageous man *does* approach you and your friend, that is your friend's cue to do something else. No man wants an audience as he awkwardly tries to introduce himself and start up a conversation.

Understand that if you make yourself approachable, you will be approachable to *all* men, not just the most desirable ones. There is nothing you can do so that just the godly, wholesome men will talk to you. If you have the light of Christ shining in you and you are approachable, men will naturally be drawn to you, whether it is a conscious or unconscious effort on their part. Some women fret over turning a man down or saying "no," but that is part of your responsibility. You have a role in this dating dance, too. You will have to distinguish between the "maybes" and the "no ways" and make an effort to handle their hearts with care.

The key to being approachable is to have fun. Men are much more likely to cross the room and talk to you if it appears that you are having a good time. Two of my single, male friends recently enrolled in a cooking class to improve their shameful cooking skills. On the first night of class, they realized that they were the only men in the room. When they were struggling to stuff their turkey, who do you think they asked for assistance? You guessed it—the two girls across the room that were laughing, smiling, and making a complete mess. Two of them have become good friends and maybe more in the future.

Go out to have fun, and you'll naturally attract men who share the same passion for life.

Be flirtatious—Like sex, flirting gets a bad rap in most Christian circles. There is a time and place for flirting just like there is a time and place for sex (and just so we are on the same page, the time and place for sex is called marriage . . .).

If by flirting, we are referring to how a woman expresses her God-given personality around the opposite sex, how she enjoys the abundant life, and how she attracts others with her heart and not just her hips, then flirt away. On the other hand, if we are referring to a woman using her voluptuous figure to arouse lust in men or win sexual favors, then she is abusing her Jedi powers. There is nothing inherently wrong with flirting if a woman's intentions are admirable. It is when flirting becomes a sport or is misleading that things get complicated.

So what exactly is admirable and permissible? Well, it depends on the situation. A couple of years ago, I had front-row seats as I watched a sweet Christian girl flirt with my roommate at a volunteer inner-city clean up. This girl partnered with my roommate as they picked up trash around the neighborhood. Being only ten yards away most of the time, I had the opportunity to hear how she engaged him in both interesting and silly conversation. After she tackled him to the ground into a pile of leaves, my roommate said he would get even with her next week. She said, "Why wait that long?" and then walked away. She had him hook, line, and sinker. He called her and took her to dinner a few days later.

Flirting doesn't need to be sexual, but it does have to be intriguing. Remember, a man can't get to know your heart and mind if he doesn't spend time with you. Give him an invitation to spend time with you. There isn't an exhaustive list of right and wrong ways to get a man's attention—what you do is a reflection of your personality and the situation. Don't be afraid to be creative and clever.

Of course, all of this advice hinges on the premise that you actually *go somewhere* and *do something*. Don't trap yourself in a mundane, stagnant life. Give your faith wings. If you want to meet new people, you have to get out of your same old routine and follow your passions, whether that entails taking a cooking class, learning to two-step, operating a power saw, or firing a handgun. And when you do notice that cute guy, wave at him . . . it may encourage him just enough to ask for your number.

Dude, It's Not That Hard

After a conference one evening, I was sitting at the dinner table with a group of women and they began joking about the cheesy pick-up lines guys use to get their attention. I cringed, just hoping they didn't mention one that I had used in the past. *You must be tired because you've been running through my mind all day! Was your father a thief?—because someone took the stars from the sky and put them in your eyes! Are you from Tennessee?—because you're the only ten I see! Pardon me, miss, I seem to have lost my phone number—could I borrow yours?*

After the roaring laughter finally subsided, the girls began discussing how they wished men would approach them. Of course, I listened intently, as if I had just sneaked into a secret society and was jotting down the cure for cancer. At the end of their conversation, it struck me—*dude, it's not that hard.*

And it really isn't. Most women aren't expecting men to perform superhuman feats to win their hearts. They simply want a confident man who displays godly characteristics and genuinely loves them. The critical word in this scenario is *confident*. As men, we need to exude a sense of true masculinity, courageous but chivalrous, powerful but humble. Like James

Bond, a confident man is never in a hurry, never surprised, and never nervous. Even when things don't go as expected, remain poised as if you anticipated the situation.

I'm not advocating being fake or putting on a show. Both men and women need to learn to be comfortable in their own skin. When you meet a dateable person, remember that you are not seeking his or her approval. Your value and position as a person have already been determined by the Lord. Don't be afraid to let your personality shine through. What the other person thinks about you is irrelevant—if you are being true to yourself and to the Lord, you have nothing to worry about.

Of course, this is always easier to write than to practice. When a guy meets a striking young lady and realizes she has a quiet but powerful spirit, he immediately starts sweating like a popsicle in a sauna. Before introducing himself, his first instinct may be to tense up or shy away. Neither of these actions is correct. He should try to behave like a duck—keep calm and unruffled on the surface, while his heart and mind paddle like mad underneath.

The cliché about first impressions is true—you never get a second chance to make a good first impression. Men, most women admit that they know within the first five minutes whether or not they want to continue the conversation or even go on a date with you. So a confident approach and mindset are critical.

Many men are at least a little nervous about talking to a woman they're interested in, and those who say they aren't are lying. So, to help you get through the first five minutes (and hopefully longer) of that initial conversation without her emotional door slamming in your face, try to remember three things:

1. Think four-to-one.

Before you say *one* thing about yourself, try to ask at least *four* questions about her. When we get nervous, many of us have a habit of rambling on and on about ourselves, and there is nothing more unattractive than a guy who constantly talks about himself. The best way to make the butterflies in your stomach disappear is to get her talking and feeling comfortable. Ask her questions and listen to her intently. There is a good chance that you two have something in common—you just have to find out what it is. The best way to figure that out is to ask her questions. Scientific studies show that on average, women speak twice as many words in a day as men do. Prove science right. Give her the opportunity to share with you.

On numerous occasions, I've watched a gentleman converse with a woman for half an hour, seldom uttering a word. When he finally gets up and excuses himself, the woman usually turns to her friends and says, "What a great guy!" And he didn't even say anything!

2. Don't vomit on her.

Don't dump too much on her too soon. When you're asking questions, try to keep the questions relatively casual and appropriate for the environment. If one of your first two questions is, "How many kids do you want?" you might as well give her the thank-you-for-voting-for-me election handshake after she responds and walk away. Her defenses are now completely up because you asked a serious, heartfelt question without building any rapport. This is *not* a good opening question. Neither are "What was your last boyfriend like?" "Why are you still single?" or "Would you like to have sex tonight?"

When you do get the opportunity to talk, speak honestly and sincerely, but don't divulge too much information or seem too eager. Let her know that you too are thoughtfully vulnerable and make her want to get to know you better. I was sitting at a restaurant in Dallas when a couple sat down at the table next to me. From their expressions and body language, it was clear that they were on a first date. The gentleman did a good job of asking questions and even got her talking about her family, of whom she was obviously very proud. But when she finished talking about her dad, the guy blurted out, "I can't wait to meet your parents." There was silence. I wanted to take him out back and beat him with a waffle iron. The rest of the evening their conversation was choppy and awkward at best. He killed any opportunity of moving forward with this girl by presuming there was a future between them. The moral of this failed dinner date is simple: Don't be too eager, Speed Racer.

3. Leave on a high note.

Always leave the first conversation with the girl wanting more. If you vomit too much information on her or talk about yourself, there is a good chance that you will go on only one date with her. But if you leave her with a sense of mystery and intrigue, then you will be perfectly positioned to take her out again.

I suggest making your first date a relatively short one so that you don't overdo it. If you take her to dinner, plan on taking her home after the meal. If things are going exceptionally well, you can always extend the date. But if you plan a long, drawn-out, romantic evening and things don't click at dinner, both of you are going to have to endure the rest of the evening. It is much wiser to have a short and powerful conversation than to talk about a million meaningless issues into the night. Leave on a high note—allow your exit at the end of the evening to be as grand as your entrance at the beginning of the evening. Like a powerfully emotional musical, allow the first act to end in suspense so that she is eager to see the second act.

In most male-female interactions, the key is not *making* things happen but *allowing* things to happen. Because we all have a natural instinct to guard our hearts, men need to make their approach casual and nonthreatening so that a woman's defenses don't spring up. And men, don't try to overthink the situation. All that women desire is for us to be the men we were designed to be. We are talking about asking a girl out on a date, not defusing a nuclear weapon. *Dude, it's not that hard. . . .*

•   •   •

When discussing godly relationships, people tend to confuse their personal beliefs with God's principles. God has made it very clear that He intends for marriage to be a sacred union where the man is the servant-leader and the woman is an equal partner,[7] but He has left much of the process of getting to this point up to interpretation. And that isn't by accident—God has done it *on purpose.* No two people, situations, and hearts are the same. There is great freedom in our romantic lives, and in many instances, God will use our individual personalities to direct our course of action. One guy may feel comfortable introducing himself to a perfect stranger at a restaurant and asking for her phone number; another may not. One woman may be forward and charismatic in "waving" at a man; another may not. These issues are not a matter of right and wrong. They are individual preferences that reflect the different personalities God has given us. As Christians, we need to be tolerant of how other people choose to date, especially fellow believers.

Despite what many of us have been taught, romantic relationships don't just *happen* to us. There is something for you to do *and* there is something for God to do. You have to step out in faith.

9

Staying Vertical

There Is Something Hormonal about Being Horizontal

*"If it wasn't for pickpockets and frisking at
the airport, I'd have no sex life at all!"*
RODNEY DANGERFIELD

In sexual relationships, everything is permissible but not everything is beneficial.[1]

Let's be honest and cut through the Christian rhetoric. If you want to have sex, you don't need your mother's, your pastor's, or even my permission. You can do it with whomever, wherever you want. You are the master of your own body and have been empowered by God to make your own decisions. But even though you *can,* you need to ask yourself if you *should.* Before you drop your drawers and assume the position, you may want to ask God what He thinks about it.

When asked a tough question about sex, Howard Hendricks, the noted professor at Dallas Theological Seminary, said, "We should not be ashamed to talk about what God was not ashamed to create." It is in this spirit that we are going to tackle the real issues that affect dating couples. Paris Hilton has no qualms about marketing her sexual escapades to the world. 50 Cent doesn't hesitate to rap about it. Even good old President Clinton has shared his promiscuous sex life with us. If those who have questionable sexual relationships aren't afraid to share, don't you think Christians ought to speak up as well? Instead of just accepting others' opinions about what we *think* sex should be, don't you think we should ask the Creator what sex was *designed* to be?

When we start talking about sex and intimacy, most of us feel a little uncomfortable. But we shouldn't. Sex is a wonderful thing! It was created by God, and He has instilled in each of us the desire to share ourselves completely and wholeheartedly with another. The sexual parts of the male and female anatomy are rich with nerve endings, suggesting that the Creator actually *wants* us to enjoy the physical experience. Sex is an amazing, heart-pounding, earth-moving, indescribable experience that can make you stumble away from the wedding bed with legs wobbling like a newborn giraffe. It is the bridge between our bodies and souls—through sex, we are granted the ability to outwardly express our inner love for one another. The reason that many of us are uncomfortable with the topic is because we are embarrassed about how we are handling it.

Many of us, Christians and non-Christians alike, have confused God's true intention for sex. On the one side, we have misunderstood the freedom He has given us by having sex outside the bonds of marriage. We have falsely assumed that what we do with our bodies is entirely up to us and that there aren't repercussions for infidelity. On the other side, we have grossly understated the importance and pleasure of sex inside a marriage relationship. God intended for a married couple to enjoy one another thoroughly, erotically, passionately, and freely. He did not intend for virginity to be a lifelong goal. The reason He drew lines in a premarital relationship is for the same reason there are lines on a football field—without them, it isn't football. It is chaos.

Great intimacy requires great commitment. If you want to be intimate with a woman, you have to be committed to her. Sex is a type of intimacy, but intimacy also includes deep levels of spiritual and emotional involvement. You don't have to touch a woman's body to touch her heart. Our culture has confused the two and instead of cultivating deep levels of intimacy, we have settled for massive amounts of sex. Because sex was designed to *feel* good, we assume that it always *is* good. But our physical pleasures, removed from the emotional and spiritual commitment, will shatter us like pain.

Think of intimacy and commitment as legs on the human body. When commitment steps forward, intimacy follows close behind. But commitment *always* has to go first. If you want to share the deepest level of physical intimacy (sex), then you need to pledge the deepest level of physical commitment (marriage). Ladies, if you really want to know why *He's Just Not That Into You*,[2] it is because you are sleeping with him! He is getting all the sex and intimacy he wants without any of the commitment. Why would he ever buy the cow if he can get the milk for free? If you'll keep your clothes on, you'll get to see if he really wants to put a ring on.

Sex is a fire. For the most part, fire is very useful and beneficial. You can use it to cook food, provide light, and warm your body. But if you take the fire out of the fireplace and place it in the middle of the living room, it will burn your house to the ground. Before you know it, the fire you once controlled will consume every room in the house. The reason that most of us have gotten burned in past relationships is because we have taken the fire out of the fireplace—we have taken sex out of marriage. We thought that a little "casual" sex couldn't hurt (by the way, what is "casual" about sharing your heart, soul, and body with someone?), but it has gotten out of hand. Our dating lives have been engulfed in flames, and our relationships have burned to the ground. Instead of being refined by the fire, we have been consumed by it.

Sex is also a ladder. With each step up the ladder, you experience a greater high. Every rung represents a new physical act you share in a relationship. Rung one, holding hands. Rung two, hugging and cuddling. Rung three, a little kiss. And so on and so forth. The higher you climb, the more physically satisfying and intimate the experience will become. However, with each step up the ladder, it becomes increasingly more dangerous. Near the top, you have far less balance, the winds of life are stronger, and the height of the fall is much greater.

So we ask ourselves: How far can we go? Where should we draw the line? How high does God allow us to climb in a dating relationship?

Believe it or not, God has given us an answer. And the answer lies in the wisdom of "everything is permissible, but not everything is beneficial."

The Sexual Ladder

When the apostle Paul wrote "everything is permissible, but not everything is beneficial," he was writing to the church at Corinth, a port city that was an intersection of many cultures and a vibrant social melting pot. In many aspects, it was the Los Angeles or New York City of its day. It was a sex-crazed environment, and Christians were struggling to be an influential part of culture without compromising their values and beliefs.

On a hill in Corinth sat the Ico-Corinthus, the temple of Aphrodite, the goddess of love. Half of the temple housed a restaurant, where people could go and have dinner. The other half housed a thousand sacred prostitutes, who engaged in sex with worshipers as part of their pagan rites.[3] As you can imagine, Christians debated whether or not to eat in the restaurant with such shameful activities going on right next door. Some believers succumbed to temptation and engaged in indecent sexual acts with the prostitutes. Others struggled to maintain their godly standards in such an ungodly environment.

Our culture and our struggle today are not very different from that of Corinth. Sex waits around every corner—on television, on the Internet, on street corners, on magazine racks—and many of us question how we should handle it. Some people think we should simply do whatever feels good. Others believe that we should remove ourselves from society and pray that God will take away our sexual desires. But neither extreme is what God intended. When Paul wrote to the

Corinthians, he understood that our sexual urges were natural and God-given, part of what makes us human. He didn't want us to separate ourselves from our culture or from sex. He simply reminded us that we shouldn't be *mastered* by our desires. He wrote, " 'Everything is permissible for me'—but not everything is beneficial. 'Everything is permissible for me'—but I will not be *mastered* by anything."[4]

We live in a culture where sex often masters us. We have all been guilty of being driven by our hormones, not our faith. What we often forget is that our bodies are a gift from God. And when God works miracles, He often works *through* His people. But if His people are not willing to honor Him with their bodies, He will not use them as vessels through which to touch this world. He will find other ways to display His mighty power.

It is critical to maintain healthy sexual boundaries because, as Christ stated, those who are pure of heart will see God.[5] If you are sleeping around, viewing pornography, or simply satisfying all your bodily hungers, you will not be able to decipher the difference between what *seems* important and what *is* important in your life. God will seem distant and irrelevant. Life will seem confusing and meaningless. Although many people deny it, our romantic endeavors have a direct impact upon our character and our faith.

In every relationship, there are three parties involved besides you and your significant other—God, your family, and your friends. Everything you say and do, and everything you don't say and do, affects these three groups. Ultimately, you and your partner make the decisions within the relationship, but those decisions need to be honoring to the Lord and sensitive to your friends and family. You are not your own, and your decisions—no matter how personal they seem—do not exist in a vacuum. God cannot bless you if you choose not to live by His principles. It's not that He doesn't want to bless you; it's just that He is not willing to compromise His perfect plan on your behalf.

Even though men and women communicate differently and exhibit different love languages, there is no excuse for not talking about your physical relationship. After you have established that you are pursuing an exclusive relationship, you need to talk about what is permissible. (Very Important Note: *Don't* discuss this on the first date! This is a conversation that should take place once you have built trust and rapport with the other person. Ideally, you would have the define-the-boundaries talk in the first couple months of dating.) Men and women often have very different views on what level of physical intimacy is appropriate while dating. You will naturally settle on the more aggressive view if you don't discuss it prior to getting hot and heavy. I hate to admit it, but a lot of men don't want to get into women's hearts—they just want to get into their pants. I'm referring to both Christian and non-Christian men alike. So, if you don't establish boundaries in the beginning, don't be surprised if there are no boundaries at all.

We often talk about "healthy sexual boundaries" in a dating relationship, but very rarely do we actually discuss what those boundaries are. Because dating wasn't a method for finding a spouse in biblical times, the Bible doesn't specifically address physical boundaries in a dating relationship. What we do know is that God specifically intended sex to be shared between a husband and wife inside the covenant of marriage. In Genesis, God states, "For this reason a man will leave his father and mother and be united to his wife, and they will become one flesh."[6] "To become one flesh" means to have sex. Did you notice that God said that the man was "to become one flesh" with his *wife?* Not his friend. Not his girlfriend. Not his mistress. With his *wife.* God designed sex to be shared only in the bond of marriage, between two people who have committed their lives to one another.

Through my own dating experiences, the wise counsel of other godly men, and my personal relationship with the Lord, I've constructed boundaries that I believe are consistent with God's design for love. The challenges that we deal with today with regard to controlling our sexual appetites are not that different from what the young believers were dealing with in Corinth. By differentiating between what is "permissible" and what is "beneficial," Paul was helping the believers establish guidelines for God-centered relationships. But please recognize that these are *guidelines,* not hard-and-fast *rules.* In order for each of us to determine "how far is too far," we have to deliberately, decisively, and continuously obey God's principles and carefully listen as He leads and guides.

When you are dating, there is freedom *in* Christ, but there is not freedom *from* Christ. You are not truly free if you remove God from the equation. Freedom is not the absence of all restrictions—it is the unbridled passion to live life within its original design. To accomplish this in a dating relationship, we need to understand the three categories of physical involvement:

1. *Permissible and beneficial (+ permissible, + beneficial).*

The physical intimacy expressed in this category can be both permissible and beneficial to a dating couple.

2. *Permissible, but not necessarily beneficial (+ permissible, – beneficial).*

You need to be in a committed relationship that has future prospects to share this kind of intimacy. While it is not necessarily bad to participate in the physical activities in this category, it is not necessarily good, either. Self-control, accountability, and respect for your partner are essential.

3. *Not permissible and not beneficial (– permissible, – beneficial).*

If you climb this high up the ladder without committing your heart to another in marriage, you are in very dangerous territory. These activities are not permissible, nor are they beneficial to a dating relationship. You are on your own if you go this far—God will not go with you.

Don't underestimate the power of physical touch. If you are an upright-walking mammal and your sexual parts are still functioning properly, there is a good chance that you have been deceived by your sexual feelings in the past. You may have dated the wrong person, shared a one-night stand, or cheated on your partner. Whatever it was, you miscalculated the power of the human touch and there have been unpleasant consequences to pay, both physically and emotionally.

Truth be told, none of us are as pure as we ought to be. Some of us have been sexually active for quite some time. Some of us just recently got involved. And some of us are thinking about it. Wherever you are, know that you are not alone. Although I've been able to refrain from having sex, I too have shared intimate moments with a woman that were neither permissible nor beneficial in God's eyes. And every time I overstepped God's boundaries, I've felt lost and confused as to how to manage my relationship.

We all have a decision to make: *Should I trust God's perfect design for my relationship?* Or *should I take matters into my own hands and follow the cultural norm?* This decision will reflect the type of love you get to experience, and ultimately, it will change your life for better or worse.

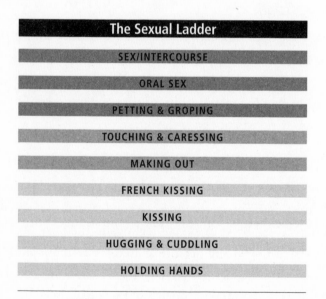

The Sexual Ladder

SEX/INTERCOURSE

ORAL SEX

PETTING & GROPING

TOUCHING & CARESSING

MAKING OUT

FRENCH KISSING

KISSING

HUGGING & CUDDLING

HOLDING HANDS

The Sexual Ladder

– Permissible, – Beneficial (Top Rungs)

  9. Sex/Intercourse

  8. Oral Sex

  7. Petting and Groping (under the clothes/without clothes)

+ Permissible, – Beneficial (Middle Rungs)

  6. Touching and Caressing (outside the clothes)

  5. Making Out

+ Permissible, + Beneficial (Bottom Rungs)

  4. French Kissing

  3. Kissing

  2. Hugging and Cuddling

  1. Holding Hands

+ Permissible, + Beneficial

New relationships are fun, but they are also very fragile. When a man first starts seeing a woman, he wants to call her, but he doesn't want to seem too anxious. The woman wants to look nice, but she doesn't want to give the impression that she's trying too hard. The man wants to be a gentleman, but he doesn't want to invade her space. The woman wants to be ladylike, but she doesn't want to come across as demanding. Because neither person really knows the stranger with whom they are sharing a soufflé, it is usually an awkward dance the first couple of dates. And then he takes her home . . .

And it becomes even more awkward! For some guys—the

ones trying not to do the horizontal mambo—the first time you walk a stunning beauty to her front door, you are sweating bullets. If you like her, you want to physically show her that you care, but what is appropriate?

This is the internal struggle that we all experience over and over again throughout dating. *What level of physical touch is appropriate with what level of emotional intimacy?*

Well, if you ask most of the dating world, you can pretty much do whatever you and your partner are comfortable with. What *Maxim, Kiss FM,* and *Desperate Housewives* forget to tell you is that *intimacy demands vulnerability.* When you become sexually intimate, you open up not only your blouse, but also your heart and mind. We act as if the physical and the emotional are not connected, but rest assured, they most definitely are. Our thoughts, feelings, and emotions are intricately interwoven, and when one part sustains damage, all sections of the body feel it.

There is nothing sexy about counseling sessions or crying yourself to sleep. That is why we see so little of it on the big screen. But most of these casual and platonic sexual relationships leave massive scars, some of which never fully heal. The media can tell you that sex helps fight depression, reduces heart disease, improves your smell, walks your dog, or whatever. The reality is that most people are simply trying to justify their own lusts and self-gratification.

If you blindly accept the idea that you can do whatever you want in life, you'll probably sleep in, eat pizza for breakfast, and grab your foxy neighbor's butt in the elevator. The reason you don't do these things is because you know you'll get fired, get fat, and get slapped—none of which sound very appealing. Our actions have consequences. Sex is no exception.

Your body is not a carnival ride. People can't just line up, take a ticket, and wait for their turn on the tilt-a-whirl. Our bodies are vessels that carry our souls, and unless somebody is willing to dive to the depths of your heart, they shouldn't be allowed to even ride the teacups. Remember, God is in you. He has etched His dream on your heart, and you deserve more than thirty minutes of pleasure with an intimate stranger.

In the early stages of a dating relationship, it is wise to approach your physical relationship slowly. Things are not always what they appear, and for better or worse, people are not always who they appear to be, especially when emotions and feelings get involved. If you don't rush into things, then you'll be able to clearly decipher whether this man sitting across from you can make the jump from "cute boy" to "soul mate."

*Rung One —Holding Hands—*As I was walking through the mall the other day, I spotted an elderly couple holding hands as they shuffled along. After watching them exchange pleasantries for a couple of minutes and talk about the clothes in the Fossil display window, I curiously approached them. I introduced myself and asked how long they had been married. Proudly, the slightly hunched-over gentleman straightened up and said, "Fifty-six years."

"What do you love most about your relationship?" I asked.

Without skipping a beat, he held up their intertwined hands and said, "You're seeing it right now."

If a happily married couple of fifty-six years says that hold-ing hands is their favorite thing to do, then there must be something quite powerful in the human touch. Don't ever rush past this rung. The first time you hold hands with a person you love, a thousand volts will rush through your body. The hair on the back of your neck will stand up. A cold shiver will run down your spine. You'll want to skip like a schoolgirl—yes, even you big old burly football players. You can put your hand on her shoulder or wrap it around her waist, but there is something simple and significant about holding her hand.

Jesus and the disciples often healed people by simply laying a hand on them. When Peter's mother-in-law lay ill with a high fever, Jesus "touched her hand" and the fever left her *immedi-ately.*[7] When you touch someone's hand, you change them instantaneously, from the inside out. Just like a slap on the wrist hurts your ego more than your carpals, a gentle touch will move your heart more than your fingers.

Gentlemen, once you marry a woman, don't ever stop holding her hand. Hold it in the grocery store, hold it in the movie theater, hold it in church. The simple effort that it takes to reach over and grasp those freshly painted nails will tell her more about your intentions than a thousand love letters. And, ladies, don't stop caressing your man's arm or squeezing his knee once the honeymoon is over. When you touch your man, you make him feel powerful. Your loving touch means as much twenty years down the road as it did when you first started dating.

While it is permissible to hold hands on the first couple of dates, it may be wise to delay the first physical encounter until you know you are interested in the other person. Besides, playing the hard-to-get, mysterious date is more of a turn-on and will ensure that the other person is really interested in getting to know you.

Rung Two—Hugging and Cuddling—Every woman I have dated has said that cuddling is her favorite thing to do. Not making out. Not sex. *Cuddling.* Who would have guessed?! Gentlemen, we don't have to worry about being porn-star husbands in bed! We simply need to perfect the art of wrapping our arms around our girls in a tender and delicate way. If you think I am wrong, ask a few of the women in your life what they think about cuddling. If they don't like it, check their pulse.

I think God designed it that way. As men, we were designed to be protectors of the family, and there is something tremendously comforting to women when we are physically present to hold them. Our embrace expresses not only our physical closeness, but our emotional closeness as well.

When you see your close friends and family, you don't just shake their hands, do you? Of course not. You hug them! Why? Because you want to convey to them that they are more than just business partners or acquaintances. They are people who hold a special place in your heart. Nothing short of a love-filled bear hug can adequately convey your care.

The same can be said about cuddling your loved one. When you hold a woman in your arms, you get to feel her heart beat against yours. Your open arms will be like a door to a magical world for your girlfriend. She can escape from all the worries, fears, heartache, and pain simply by running into your arms. If you ever get in an argument with your girl, before you say one word in your defense, hold her in your arms for a couple minutes. It will alleviate the tension and remind you that she is beautifully fragile. When you feel her body and sense her pain, you will speak much more gently.

For the most part, hugging and cuddling are very innocent and harmless ways to share intimacy with someone else. But like any gift, your powers can lead you to the Dark Side of the Force if you are not careful, young Jedi. A hug good night at the end of a date or a little snuggling on the couch during a movie is certainly permissible when you are dating. But don't use this as justification to allow your girlfriend of four days to lie directly on top of you during the whole three-hour *Braveheart* flick.

Rung Three—Kissing—I'm not talking about locking lips and sharing spit at this point. I'm simply referring to a quick peck on the lips or the cheek. Don't get all scientific on me here—I don't know exactly how long a quick kiss is, whether it is one second or five. However, I'll warn you that if you press your lips together for too long, you are going to skip right over the break-the-ice kiss to the take-a-deep-breath French kiss. Don't be in a hurry to jump this rung. There is ineffable charm that comes with slow dancing up the ladder.

The art of kissing your date on the hand, cheek, or lips is a lost talent. Most men and women seem to jump over this rung for the hot and heavy French kissing. But you can win some real bonus points for dropping a quick kiss on your date's cheek after a romantic evening. Men like women who play a little hard to get, who are guarding their hearts, and women like men who have self-control. It adds mystery and intrigue to a blossoming relationship. If you just shared a wonderful evening with a beautiful young lady, don't hesitate to give her a little kiss. It will make both of your hearts flutter.

Dr. Laura Berman of Chicago's Berman Center states, "Married couples often come into my office and say their relationship is failing, and I ask them, 'When is the last time you kissed?' People will say, 'Well, we don't kiss, except when we have sex.' " Her Rx: smooch every day—it will bring the connection back to the relationship.

But remember, timing is everything when it comes to kissing. Chris Rock likens it to double-dutch. You try to get in too early—you get tangled in the ropes. You try to get in too late—you get tangled in the ropes. You have to time your jump just right.

Rung Four—French Kissing—Or what many refer to as "real kissing." If you think about it, shouldn't it be called Hebrew kissing? France wasn't declared a nation until 1789, and I'm sure that this type of lip-locking exercise was taking place in Jerusalem back in the time of Jesus. But for argument's sake, we'll give the French the credit for it right now— God knows they can use some positive publicity.

Our culture has downplayed the erotic nature of the French kiss. Many celebrities smooch everybody they want and don't think twice about it. (From a health standpoint, it may be safer to lick the tire of a farm tractor than to kiss your favorite movie star.) But a kiss is so much more than a casual greeting. I can honestly say that I've never had a first kiss where I didn't have butterflies doing circus tricks in my stomach. There is just something very sensual about two sets of lips coming together.

If there is a physical indicator that more than friendship is developing, then tongue wrestling should be that sign in most relationships. Both parties should be interested in pursuing a more committed relationship to share this level of intimacy.

On the other hand, a tongue-locked kiss doesn't necessarily mean she is going to marry you or bear your children. There is the false romantic fantasy circling in the Christian realm that the kiss seals the deal. While your heart may jump and do an Olympic swan-dive back into your chest, there are still many important nonphysical issues to address before sending out "save-the-date" cards. A kiss doesn't mean everything.

There is often confusion among the genders about what French kissing really means. Princes often view kissing as mere physical pleasure while princesses usually see kissing as a stepping stone to a more serious relationship. Kip and Rachael are a perfect example. When Kip decided to end a romantic evening with Rachael by playing tonsil hockey, he assumed that it was merely an exclamation point on the end of a wonderful date. Rachael, however, took the kiss to mean that Kip wanted an exclusive and committed relationship.

There was confusion because Kip and Rachael, like most couples, had very different views of what level of intimacy is appropriate with what level of commitment. Because Kip didn't communicate to her that their kiss was simply a "thank you" for a wonderful evening, Rachael can't be faulted for assuming that he wanted to pursue an exclusive relationship. All the confusion could have been avoided if they would have honestly communicated their feelings and intentions. Their situation is a good example of why not to rush into the intimacy of French kissing until you are prepared for the commitment that accompanies it. Kip could have avoided the confusion and shown his appreciation for a wonderful evening by simply giving her a peck on the cheek. Don't rush to rung four when rung three will do the job.

Many people ask me if it is appropriate to French kiss on the first date. Well, it depends. If you have known the person for longer than just one evening, it may be appropriate to share lipstick. But if this is your first evening with her, you should wait until you get to know her better. We all put our best foot forward on the first date. Wait and see what happens on the second and third date. Once you get to know and are attracted to a person's true heart, then pucker up. You'll never get yourself into trouble by waiting too long to kiss, but you can certainly cause drama if you kiss too soon.

Most important, make it count. Everybody remembers their first "real" kiss.

+ Permissible, − Beneficial

One spring break when I was in college, a group of us guys decided to take a road trip to the Grand Canyon. For some undefined medical reason, the thought of trekking halfway across the country to see the world's largest hole seemed more appealing than lying on the beach with a bunch of beautiful ladies. So, underfunded and unprepared, we packed up the minivan (yes, I actually had to drive a minivan to college) and headed west.

After about eighteen hours in the Aerostar, we arrived at the giant crack in the ground. It wasn't the first crack I had experienced on my spring break as two of my heavyset football buddies slept face down, shorts gangster style, most of the trip. As we walked along the edge of the canyon, we made a very concerted effort to stay a good distance away from the ledge. Personally, I'm not afraid of heights, but there are unpredictable wind gusts at the top and the average depth of the canyon is over five thousand feet. I didn't have any desire for the next day's headline to read—*Ex-Tight End and Two Linemen Fall to Their Deaths in Canyon Accident.*

As we debated about whether or not to hike to the bottom, a family with three small kids approached us. Two of the kids held tightly to their parents' hands, but one squirrelly, psychotic kid made a beeline right for the edge of the canyon. When his dad realized what he was doing, the foot race was on. The kid darted for the edge. The dad darted for the kid. We made bets on who would get there first.

Fortunately, the dad caught up with his training Olympic sprinter right before he got to the edge. He grabbed his son by the arm, pulled him a safe distance away from the edge, and said, "Son, you have to be careful. There is no railing here and the canyon is about a mile deep. Trust me, the canyon looks just as beautiful from a couple steps back as it does from the edge and there is less risk of falling in."

Trust me, your physical relationship will look just as beautiful from a couple steps back as it does from the edge, and there is less risk of falling in.

Our bodies are truly God's greatest creations, fashioned in His likeness.[8] But much like the canyon, we have to draw certain boundaries in a dating relationship so that we don't fall victim to an unexpected gust or a slip of the foot. Naturally, we want to run right to the beauty, but the Father has gently grabbed us by the arm and said, "Child, be careful." The heights are magnificent, but the depths are perilous.

Much of God's guidance in dating relationships, especially the physical aspects, can be summed up in one phrase:

Draw a line and take a step back.

Simply stated, you have to figure out what God intended for your relationship and then take a step back so that when you stumble—and you *will* stumble—you don't fall into the canyon. Your partner will look just as beautiful from a couple of steps back.

To apply this wisdom to the ladder, prayerfully discern which rung you feel comfortable ascending to and then choose the rung right underneath it. For example, if you feel God urging you to do no more than make out (rung five), then you need to stop at French kissing (rung four). If you set your boundaries below your true comfort point, you will leave room for failure if things get too passionate and pleasurable. If you push toward the edge of your comfort zone and draw the line at making out, you will be disappointed, guilt-ridden, and hurt if you fall into touching and caressing (rung six).

In an ideal world, we wouldn't do more than French kiss before getting married. We would restrict our physical activities to those things that are clearly both permissible and beneficial in God's eyes. But as a relationship becomes more committed over time, there are certain situations where it is permissible for a couple to be more intimate.

Please understand something. I'm writing this to you as a concession, not as a command from the Lord. I don't want you to burn with passion, but I also don't want you to make a foolish, uneducated decision to marry someone simply because your hormones have taken control of your brain. There are far too many Christian couples who are getting married in twelve months or less simply because their pants are on fire. When things don't work out, they each say the other person isn't godly, point to Scripture to defend their stance, divorce one another, and walk away sad but temporarily sexually satisfied. This tragic turn of events can be even more detrimental to our faith than a couple who is overly physical in a dating relationship. So, before you rush into a foolish marriage or a really stupid sexual relationship, you may want to educate yourself on the things that are permissible but not always beneficial.

Rung Five—Making Out—If French kissing is a sprint, then making out is a marathon. Many couples have make-out sessions that need to be timed with a sundial.

While kissing just includes the art of lip-locking with one another, making out encompasses kissing around other sensual parts of the body such as the neck and ears. In the makeout phase, couples are more active with their hands, often gently touching one another's face and head. (However, making out does *not* include roaming hands that caress sexual parts of the body, either inside or outside someone's clothes.)

Moving from rung four to rung five can be a very effortless step, so you have to be conscious of what you are doing. Sometimes you go in for a kiss and it is just so dang enjoyable that you decide to camp there for a while. Making out is not necessarily good or bad—it just depends on the situation.

The key to mastering the physical is establishing your boundaries before the relationship starts. Because once you are knee-deep in passion, your intellect shuts down and you revert to your primal instincts. If there are no boundaries in place, making out becomes a no-holds-barred game of naked Twister.

A good rule to remember: If making out becomes the *point* of you two getting together, then you are heading down the wrong road. Making out should be only an outward expression of your mutual inward development. Making out is the icing on the cake, not the cake itself. You shouldn't have to kiss or make out every time you get together. If you are in a maturing relationship with future potential and you are both comfortable being this physically intimate, then you may be able to make out with one another and still glorify God in the process. But be cautious, this can be a slippery slope.

Rung Six—Touching and Caressing (outside the clothes)—Is it getting hot in here or is it just me? Whhhheeewwwwww. . . .

Okay, I've increased the size of my inbox so that the thousands of irate pastors and upset parents can e-mail me about how I shouldn't be encouraging you to touch one another's bodies. So just for the record—I'm not encouraging you. In fact, I hope and pray that you will keep your hands to yourself as much as possible. If you just have to be physical with each other, go for a jog.

But most of us aren't doing that, are we? According to statistics, sixty-five percent of women and sixty-eight percent of men have had intercourse by the time they are eighteen years old.[9] In other words, almost seven out of ten of us—whether we are Christian or not—have given our bodies to someone else by the time we are legal adults here in the U.S. Suddenly, a little touching doesn't seem like such a big deal.

But it is a big deal. Sexual activity is a ladder, and once you step up one rung, you have the incredible urge to conquer the next one. And the next one. And the next one. Soon, you're approaching the top of a dangerous climb, and all you set out to do was steal a little kiss.

As a single, dating young adult, I know how difficult it is to stop climbing the ladder. I, too, often have moments when I just want to tear my girlfriend's clothes off. But I continually remind myself (and am continually reminded by my friends and accountability partner) that God has my best interests in mind and that sex is the most passionate and fulfilling when it is shared with someone who has devoted her life to you.

We often falsely assume that this physical battle is new and unique to our generation. But it isn't. The Corinthians struggled with these same issues and that is why Paul told them, "It is good for a man not to touch a woman."[10] The word *touch* means to light a fire, or to arouse sexual passion or activity.[11] Paul wasn't saying that it is inappropriate to hold a woman's hand, touch her leg, or give her a backrub. But he was saying that you have to be very careful how you touch a woman so that you don't arouse a strong and *uncontrollable* sense of sexual passion in her. *Uncontrollable* is the key word here. He knew that women are like Crock-Pots. They take a while to heat up, but once they are hot, they are nearly impossible to cool down.

So be very careful how you touch and caress one another, and don't even think about removing a piece of clothing to do it. I know that there are moments in a dating relationship when it feels like all the planets have aligned—the dinner is *ah magnific!*, your date looks hotter than summer car seats, the radio serenades both of you with a little Michael Bublé, your lightly spritzed scent becomes a powerful aphrodisiac, the house whispers intimacy, and the couch transforms into a soft cloud of blankets. When it gets to this boiling point, keep your hands on the outside of her clothes and away from her private parts. Once clothes start coming off, it is nearly impossible to stop. God will never give you more than you can handle, but don't try to handle more than He has given you.

– Permissible, – Beneficial

If you have climbed this far up the ladder, you are not in Kansas anymore, Dorothy. This isn't a dream where you can wake up and everything will be just fine. You have stumbled into an area that is not permissible or beneficial. It is not blessed by God.

Yeah, I know, you like it and she likes it. Besides, you have both verbally agreed that your relationship is not about the physical stuff anyway. So what's the big deal? Well, there is something going on beneath the surface that you need to know about. Your body is making promises that your heart is not ready to keep.

Culture tries to tell us that the body and the soul are not intricately interconnected, but they most certainly are. Your feelings, thoughts, and emotions are directly affected by your body's activities. Sex can't be casual, because sex isn't informal, careless, or accidental. Even when it is spontaneous, you still have to consciously think about taking your clothes off—it doesn't just magically happen. Not only do you become physically naked during sex, but you become emotionally and spiritually naked as well. A connected sexual experience is a gateway to your soul.

Between rung six and rung seven, God intended for a couple to get married. When two lovers devote their lives to one another, God yells, "Climb on!" and they have the freedom to enjoy all the blessings of the last three steps. God designed it this way because He knew you would be completely vulnerable at the top of the ladder. Toward the peak of the climb, there is nothing to hold on to, the ladder is much more unstable, and you are easily affected by the winds of life. When you enter into a Christ-centered marriage, though, God becomes the safety net around the ladder. He can help you and your spouse through emotional, spiritual, and physical challenges of marriage because you are operating within His preordained framework. You don't have that type of reassurance in a dating relationship. If you decide to climb outside of the physical boundaries that He has established for you, the first thing you will feel if you fall won't be His hand, but the ground.

If you are in a sexually active dating relationship above rung six, you are acting on your own accord outside of God's will. Don't be surprised if a person sleeps with you one night and then tells you he doesn't like you the very next day. You are swimming in dangerous, shark-infested waters with cement shoes. If you truly don't want to awaken or arouse sexual love until you have a committed partner, I have two words for you: *Stay Vertical.*

Stay Vertical

There is something hormonal about being horizontal. Although it has yet to be proven scientifically, hormones seem to rush to your head and take over when you lie down. Every single person I talk to about this first stumbled sexually when they were lying down. Think about it, how many people do you know who had sex the first time standing up?!

Staying vertical is the checks-and-balance system for avoiding physical temptation. Since we *are* human and we *do* have sexual urges, it is important to not let our fleshly desires get the best of us. You can say the most eloquent prayer imaginable and quote the entire book of Deuteronomy in Hebrew, but once you are naked with a girl, you might as well be quoting the Yellow Pages. You are doing no good, because in reality, you don't want the pleasure to stop. To avoid things getting this far, you need to stay vertical.

Through all my years of dating, this simple rule has never failed me. It works in nearly every circumstance. For example . . .

- If you start passionately making out with someone while standing up, your first instinct is to find a place to sit or lie down. Stay vertical.
- If you are going to lie down and watch a movie with your date but your real intentions are just to get physical . . . stay vertical.
- If your significant other wants you to spend the night so that you can make out between the sheets, stay vertical. (You won't sleep much standing up!)

Physical contact makes you weak in the knees, and the first thing you want to do is sit or lie down. Don't. Stay vertical and compose yourself. Once your mind and heart have wrestled control away from your hormones, then you can sit down.

I'm not saying that you can't ever lie down with your girlfriend. I'm simply saying that staying vertical is an excellent way to fight off the urge to get naked. When you are vertical, your hands are less likely to wander, and you get tired quicker. If you etch this alert in your mind before passion runs amok, you can avoid doing something that you will later regret.

Staying vertical is about exercising self-control. When you get married, you aren't immediately removed from all the sexual temptations and struggles you had when you were single. Far from it. You'll still get bombarded with erotic images from the Internet, television, and the opposite sex, and you have to possess the discipline not to succumb to your throbbing hormones. Marriage isn't magic, and God doesn't sprinkle you with fairy dust after the vows to make you immune from sexual temptations. The self-control you develop—or *don't* develop—in a dating relationship will carry over into your marriage. It will help you navigate the unpredictable waters of sex, even those moments when your wife says she is just "not in the mood."

Staying vertical is not just a physical reminder, but a spiritual reminder as well. When you keep your focus on God— when you think vertically—you are more concerned about what glorifies Him than what gratifies you. If you focus on your vertical relationship with God, He will take care of your horizontal relationships with other people. It is easy in a romantic situation to turn all your energies toward the person you are dating and neglect both God and your loved ones. Keep your heart focused on Him, and your passions, both sexual and emotional, will be held in check.

Vertical Limit

When you ascend to rung six, you have reached the *vertical limit* in your physical relationship. In mountain climbing, the vertical limit is twenty-four thousand feet. It refers to the altitude at which the oxygen-deprived human brain begins to deteriorate and lose its ability to make reliable judgments. When you climb over the vertical limit, you slowly begin to die and you don't even know it. If you stay above twenty-four thousand feet without the assistance of an oxygen tank, it is just a matter of time until your entire body shuts down.

In a dating relationship, the vertical limit on the sexual ladder is rung six, touching and caressing. When you climb over that, the intense physical nature of the relationship slowly begins to impair reliable judgment. Your relationship will begin to deteriorate, and slowly but surely, your romance will begin to die. You can stave it off for a little while, but unless you descend quickly, you are doomed. You will either catapult into a full-blown sexual relationship or you will end up destroying your romance.

We are not meant to climb over rung six without the assistance of marriage. Most of us instinctively know that we have reached the vertical limit because we begin to feel queasy and a little sick to our stomachs. Some people call this guilt but it is actually our bodies (and the Holy Spirit) warning us of impending danger. If we ignore these early warning signs, we will slowly become numb to our actions until we don't feel anything at all. At this stage, spiritual death is imminent. God will not continue to speak to us if we insist on living outside of His perfect will.

Many of us have climbed to the top of the ladder while dating and have experienced the death of our hearts. The very thing that we thought would save us, the deepest level of physical intimacy, was the thing that shattered our dreams.

Rung Seven—Petting and Groping (under the clothes/ without clothes)—When you are on rung six, your mind is still somewhat clear and you are gently touching and caressing the other person in intimate ways. When you leap to rung seven, however, your spiritual mind begins to shut down and caressing turns into petting and groping, much more animal-like behaviors. Instead of thinking about what is best for the other person, you begin thinking about how good this feels and how much more you can get.

Ladies, if a guy is anxious to put his hands all over you, he doesn't really respect you. Some guys don't really want a girlfriend. They want pleasure. A girlfriend is just the necessary apparatus for receiving that pleasure. If a guy tells you he loves you during a physical act, it doesn't count. If he really loves you, he should be able to tell you when he doesn't have his hands on your butt. Many times guys will whisper sweet nothings in women's ears to manipulate them into becoming more physical. Be cautious. Be smart. If a red flag comes up, don't ignore it.

Many guys want you to cry out, "Oh, God!" but not in a way that is glorifying to the One above. When he has his hands up your shirt, I can guarantee that he is not thinking about what is best for you. If he was, he wouldn't have roaming hands. He is concerned only with how much pleasure he can receive. Because the primary love language of most guys is physical touch, you are in real hot water if you take him to the bedroom. It is easy for a little sexual fondling to turn into sex.

Gentlemen, this is the rung where you get the opportunity to stand up and be real men. Instead of making the women the keepers of the physical boundaries, show some authority and self-control and put a stop to things if clothes start to come off. There is nothing more attractive to a godly woman than a man who can deny his own bodily hunger for the overall good of the relationship. We can begin the transformation from passive men back to powerful leaders if we start controlling our hormones. From personal experience, I know that this is the point where I can either continue to climb up and make the relationship about me, or I can climb down and make it about God.

The last three rungs on the ladder are made of ice. They are exceptionally slippery, and if you are not careful, you can easily stumble into sex. You can use whatever excuse you like— "we love each other," "everyone else is doing it," "it is just this once"—but caressing each other's sexual parts during a dating relationship is not appropriate. Even though it may *feel* good, it is not part of a God-designed dating relationship. When you climb dangerously over the vertical limit, you risk destroying your relationship with your partner and distancing yourself from God.

Rung Eight—Oral Sex—Last summer, I was having dinner with Jessie, a good Christian buddy and a respected businessman, when he said something that made both my sushi and my jaw drop. Staring down at his plate, he whispered, "Marci and I just had an abortion."

From an outsider's perspective, Jessie and Marci were the perfect couple. Jessie was an ex-collegiate baseball player who decided to forgo a professional career and start his own business. An excellent communicator, he was a leader not only in his community but also in his church. Marci was amazing as well. Constantly barraged by opportunities to model, she chose a different path and pursued a career in teaching. She wanted to have an impact on children's lives and believed she could do it by showing them her inner beauty, not just her outer beauty. Jessie and Marci met their junior year in college while serving with a campus ministry. I met them shortly thereafter and had enjoyed watching them date for over three years. To say I was shocked at the news was an understatement.

"What happened?" I asked.

"Well," he started, "we made some poor decisions. We knew we needed to wait until we were married to have sex, but we thought everything besides sex was okay. We started going down on one another about five months ago, and at first, just loved it. But we started to want more and more, and finally, we just broke down and had sex."

Stunned by everything that was happening and amazed by his candor, I was still confused as to how they made the leap from oral sex to sex. "But how did it get all the way to sex?" I asked.

Lifting up his head for the first time in the whole conversation, he looked me straight in the eyes and spoke firmly as if to warn me: "Listen, when you go that far physically in a relationship—when you start pleasuring one another in various ways—you begin to feel completely comfortable. Slowly, but surely, you let down all your defenses, all your guards, and you begin to justify everything because you are 'in love.' In the end, there is nothing stopping you . . . nothing between you and sex."

As Jessie was talking, my jaw dropped down to my spleen. I couldn't believe what I was hearing. But as he explained how they failed to guard their hearts,[12] to flee from sexual temptation,[13] or to "draw a line and take a step back," I came to a terrifying realization. . . . It could have been me. Or you. Or any of us. Like many young dating couples, he and Marci longed for nothing more than to love and be loved. But there was one tragic flaw in their physical relationship that unwound the whole ball of romance—they chose to do things their way, not God's.

If you choose to climb the ladder to the area that is neither permissible nor beneficial while dating, know that God will not bless your relationship. It's not that He doesn't want to. He just won't change his perfect plan for love and marriage to suit your lustful desires. God designed our physical relationships to be a natural, progressive, important part of dating, but the last three rungs were specifically set apart for marriage. The reason that the last three are grouped together is because they are interconnected, and it is very easy for one thing to lead to another.

Jessie found this out the hard way. Once he and Marci started petting each other's naked bodies, the natural next step was oral sex. And once they started having oral sex, the natural next step was intercourse. By not drawing a line and taking a step back, they left themselves no margin for error, and now they are struggling to deal with the consequences that come from operating outside of God's will.

Even though intercourse and oral sex are two different and distinct acts, it is very hard to separate the two. Both involve taking off clothes, interacting with genitalia, and reaching orgasm. Both increase the risk of contracting a sexually transmitted disease (STD). It's alarming to read that two-thirds of all new STD infections occur among young people under the age of twenty-five and there are fifteen million new cases in the U.S. each year. (If that doesn't scare you enough, more than sixty-five million people in the U.S.—approximately one-fourth of the general population—currently have an incurable STD.[14]) Both provide a false sense of emotional and physical security inside a dating relationship because the level of intimacy doesn't match the level of commitment. Most important, both ignore God's principles and can cause serious heartache if shared outside of marriage. The Bible states, "All other sins a man commits are outside his body, but he who sins sexually sins against his own body . . . the temple of the Holy Spirit."[15]

The reason many of us don't see the problem with oral sex in a dating relationship is because we don't call it what it is— a sin. We refer to it as a "growing experience, a natural part of dating, an experiment, or a mistake." A mistake is when you put on two mismatching socks, not when you wind up without your SpongeBob SquarePants boxers in a woman's bedroom. If we would call it what it is, we would see that it is a clear violation of God's standard, and we wouldn't be so comfortable with our actions. When we see a woman prostitute her body for money, we know it is wrong. But many of us, both men and women alike, are prostituting our bodies for pleasure. We are called to honor God with our bodies, and when we don't, it is nothing less than a sin.[16]

Of course, our culture tries to tell us that there is nothing wrong with engaging in this type of intimacy. If you are in a slump that makes the L.A. Clippers look like NBA Championship contenders, feel free to pick up *Hilary* magazine and learn the best places to give your boyfriend a blow job. Or pick up *FHM* and learn how to find your girlfriend's G-spot. Our sexual appetites are never satisfied, and we always long for more, more, more. But when this level of intimacy is disconnected from a God-ordained marriage, you may learn like Jessie did that more isn't always better. You may get more sex, but you may also get more heartache, more confusion, more shame, and more guilt. Like intercourse, oral sex is not an essential ingredient for a successful dating relationship. No case of orally denied spontaneous combustion has been reported among couples in love. But don't just take my word on it. Read about it for yourself in the Bible. Talk to God about it. If you do, you'll find that ignoring God's principles is about as wise as trying to lick the frost off a cold lamppost. You may get yourself stuck to something you don't really want.

Rung Nine—Intercourse—When *Sex and the City* first aired, Carrie and her friends were all single. Tired of trying to be the perfect mate for some Prince Charming who never showed up, they decided it was better to just start having sex like men do—casual, platonic, meaningless sex. But after six seasons, numerous flings, a few boyfriends, countless pairs of Manolo Blahniks, some small issues, and many Mr. Big issues, Carrie was *still* single. You know why? Because she kept engaging in meaningless, commitment-less sex!

The best way to extinguish a burning relationship is to have sex. Once a man knows he can have sex without any responsibilities, why would he ever commit to a long-term relationship?

In Los Angeles and other "progressive" cities throughout the country, there is an unspoken rule among many singles: After three dates, you need to have sex with your partner to see if you are physically compatible. This may be the most thoughtless, superficial, asinine, heartless, disgusting, ridiculous, impractical, juvenile rule I have ever heard of! If you believe this rule, please hit your call button so that the flight attendant can come back and whack you with a tack hammer. What part of "lifelong commitment" do you not understand?!

And when I say commitment, I'm referring to marriage. Having your boyfriend sign a three-page monogamy contract and put a down payment on your ring doesn't count. There *is* a difference between having sex and making love. If you are bumping and grinding in a dating relationship, you are simply having sex. You are gratifying your own desires in a selfish, shallow, primal manner. You may love the person you are with, but you are not expressing it within God's provision; you are sharing deep physical intimacy without deep physical commitment. On the other hand, when you make love to your spouse, you are physically expressing with your body what your heart has already committed to—eternity.

God designed sex to create a special bond between two people. The monstrosity of sexual intercourse outside of marriage is that those who indulge in it are trying to isolate one kind of union (the sexual) from all the other kinds of union— the emotional, the intellectual, and the spiritual—which were intended to go along with it.[17] God said that "the two will become one flesh," meaning that there would be not only a physical bond, but a spiritual and emotional bond would develop as well.[18] All parts of your being are interconnected and it is absurd to think otherwise.

If you don't believe what Scripture says about it, at least examine what happens to a person physiologically. In women, sex releases a flood of hormones, oxytocin and dopamine being two of them. Oxytocin, the same hormone that women release while breast feeding, makes a woman feel close to her partner. Dopamine makes her feel more content in his embrace. So even if a girl thinks she can have casual sex with no regrets, she will feel emotionally involved and intimately vulnerable after the act. Her body will remind her what her head and heart already know—sex is sacred.

Having sex outside of marriage is like peeling an onion. If you continue to strip off the layers, ultimately there will be nothing left. Despite what our culture may say, sex is not a basic human need. Food is. Shelter is. Oxygen is. Sex isn't. I've never seen a man's head explode from lack of sex.

If you want to find a prince or princess, follow the rule of royalty: Kiss the frogs in your life. Don't take them to bed.

.   .   .

We don't need more sex in our lives—we need more life in our sex. Before we enjoy the sex of love, we need to practice the patience of love, the kindness of love, the discipline of love, the vulnerability of love, and the commitment of love. We need to understand the meaning, not just the mechanics, of our relationships. Everybody wants a romantic, fairy-tale type of marriage, but very few of us are willing to do the things required to achieve it. If you want your relationship to be different than the myriad of failing romances out there, you have to live it differently. You can't expect to have a special marriage relationship if you don't have a special dating relationship.

Many of us have sabotaged ourselves by mishandling the physical aspect of our romances. Intimacy is a natural, progressive, important part of dating, but commitment must always precede intimacy as you climb the sexual ladder. If there is a gap between intimacy and commitment, it creates room for disappointment and heartache. Ask yourself this question: Is it sex you desire, or is it closeness, affection, and affirmation?

Almost all of us have made sexual mistakes that we are not proud of. Some of us have guilt. Some have shame. Some have fear. But Christ died to give us another chance. It is never too late to start again. If you want to continue playing chicken with a train, feel free to ignore God's principles. But if you are truly interested in developing an emotionally satisfying and sexually fulfilling relationship, there is a better way.

Stay back. Stay vertical. And most important, stay close to God.

10

More "Buts" Than a Nudist Colony

Your Relationship Is *Not* the Exception to the Rule

"You come to love not by finding the perfect person, but by seeing an imperfect person perfectly."

SAM KEEN

When it comes to relationships, everybody thinks that they are the exception to the rule. *I know God desires this, but . . . That's really good advice, but . . . I meant to handle the situation that way, but . . .* While I'll concede that every situation is unique and every couple is different, we all struggle with the same things to one degree or another. There is nothing new under the sun. God does understand and empathize with your situation, *but* He is not going to change His perfect and all-encompassing plan so that you can gratify your every desire. We have to learn to fit into God's plan, not the other way around.

I've received a number of thought-provoking questions over the last couple of years. Hopefully, these real-life situations will speak to your heart the same way they spoke to mine.

Dear Jason,

My boyfriend and I have been dating for about a year, and we just recently started talking about getting married. I really like this guy a lot! He has a great job, comes from a great family, and even goes to church with me every week. My lease is coming up on my apartment next month, and he suggested that we just move in together to save up for the wedding. It may be a good way to get to know each other's little habits before tying the knot. What do you think?

Cindy H.
Spokane, WA

)(

Dear Getting Ready to Play House,

Before you bubble-wrap your skimpies and load the U-haul, you may want to prayerfully consider whether moving in with Prince Charming is a good idea. Yeah, it may sound fun and exciting, but is it in your best interest? Data shows that over five million people in the U.S. alone are currently cohabitating, even though couples that live together have twice the breakup rate of married couples.[1] When you cohabitate, you are sliding, not deciding, into a relationship.

When we were kids, we used to play house (well . . . I didn't, but . . . okay . . . fine, I did . . .). It was fun because we got to experience all the benefits—the dinners, the games, the conversations—without any of the responsibilities. When dating couples live together, they are just big kids playing house again. Living together increases the level of physical, emotional, and spiritual intimacy without increasing the overall level of commitment, creating a dangerous imbalance. And if you are struggling not to get naked with him now—which you probably are if you really love him—then the pressure will be tenfold when you see each other walking around the house in your pajamas.

Women often see cohabitating as a step toward marriage while men tend to see it as an optional step before full commitment. So even though it sounds logical, living together before marriage is often very detrimental. Besides, if he really has a great job, then a few more months of separate housing isn't going to bankrupt you. The long-term blessings you will receive from the Lord will far outweigh the short-term financial benefit.

—JBI

Dear Jason,

I'm twenty-seven years old, and I'm proud to say that I'm still a virgin. I've had the opportunity to date a couple of godly young men, but they weren't virgins, and I feel that God is telling me to wait for a virgin. I think I deserve it. What do you think?

Melissa P.
Phoenix, AZ

Dear Proud One,

You may hear a voice speaking to you, but I can guarantee that it isn't God's. When people find out that I'm a virgin, they assume that I'm waiting to marry a virgin. But what kind of sense does that make? Who am I to decide what is best for me? More poignantly, who am I to hold someone's past against them? God has forgiven me for numerous sins, and I'm called to pay that same grace forward. Paul was very clear that "love makes no list of wrongs."[2] And if you make a decision not to date someone simply because they have had sex, you are holding their sins against them. Do you need to be cautious and make sure his sexual conquests are not a reflection of his heart? Absolutely. Do you need to engage him in a serious and personal conversation to make sure he doesn't have an STD or any children? Without a doubt. But you can't judge his heart based on his past. How would you feel if a man rejected you because you used to struggle with jealousy? Or anger? Or loneliness? Remember, the standard that you measure unto others will be measured unto you. What goes around, comes around.

Don't limit who God is trying to bring into your life. I've learned far more about unconditional love from women whose past experiences were vastly different from mine than those who walked a similar path. Besides, those who are forgiven much, love much. Your concern should be focused on where his heart is now instead of where it was five years ago.

I commend you on your physical obedience, but you

don't *deserve* a virgin husband. I don't *deserve* a virgin wife. What we *deserve* died with Christ upon the cross.

—JBI

Dear Jason,

I need a little help. When I went off to college two years ago, I met this really sweet (and cute) boy named Matt. I thought it was a God-send when I found out that our dorm rooms were right next to each other. Since we were both new to the school, we immediately became close friends. He made it very clear that he was a Christian and attended Bible study almost every week. We have never "officially" dated, but from time to time, he asks me to dinner and the night usually ends with a make-out session. I really enjoy spending time with him, but he says that he doesn't want to ruin the great friendship we have. Do you think he'll ever think of me as a girlfriend and not just a friend?

Candy R.
Shreveport, LA

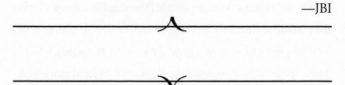

Dear Let's Make This Official,

Nope—he'll never consider you a girlfriend because he is getting all the physical and emotional intimacy he wants without any of the commitment. If he can call you whenever he has nothing better to do on a Friday night and you'll run into his arms, why would he ever build a real relationship with you? He may manipulate the situation by saying that he is "protecting the friendship," but he is really just "protecting his own butt." Be honest with yourself—you are really just friends with benefits. And this relationship is exceptionally convenient for him.

If you want to see if he is really serious about you, turn him down the next couple times he invites you to dinner-and-a-make-out-session. If he really wants to pursue you, he'll appreciate you guarding your heart and playing a little hard to get. Men like challenges, and we are hard-wired to battle for the heart of a beautiful princess. We assume that if there is no battle, then there is nothing of real value behind the castle walls. Don't just roll over on command. You have too much to offer. And if he doesn't pursue you, he isn't interested. You will then have made room for the men who are.

—JBI

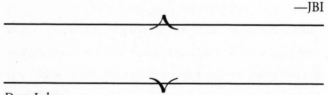

Dear J-dog,

I hear what you are saying about saving sex for marriage, but I'm not sure that I agree. I mean, if I'm going to buy a car, I'm going to take it for a test drive before I shell out the big bucks. What if I marry this girl and she is terrible in bed? If God is good and wants what is best for me, He can't possibly want me to marry someone who doesn't sexually satisfy me. You hear me barking, big dog?

Jamaal A.
Los Angeles, CA

Dear Test Driving,

I hear you barking, big dog. I don't want to marry a woman who doesn't sexually satisfy me, either. But here is the thing—the reason that so many men are unsatisfied in their sexual relationships is because they are test-driving all the cars! It has become a matter of comparison. And comparison is cancer for the soul. Does Aubrey drive better than Mandy? Does Angela drive better than Lynda? If you haven't driven a car before, any car that you drive will handle like a sportster. Why? Because you don't know any better! You'll have an amazing sexual experience because you haven't established unrealistic expectations.

If you are currently taking cars out for a spin, STOP! You'll be amazed at how much better your future sex life will be. More important, you'll be reminded of its place in your relationship. Physical intimacy grows out of emotional and spiritual intimacy. It is a natural progression when you get to know a woman's heart. I have yet to meet a couple who has cultivated spiritual intimacy with each other and with the Lord who isn't sexually satisfied in their relationship. Once your hearts and eyes have met, bringing your hips together will be easy.

—JBI

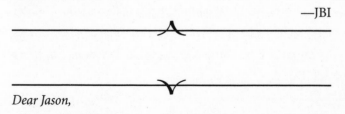

Dear Jason,

Why should I listen to you?! You've never even had sex, but you think you can tell the rest of us how we should handle our sex lives?! Don't you think you ought to keep your mouth shut until you have a little experience?

Amanda M.
New York, NY

X

Dear Too Many Frappuccinos,

Whoa! Take a deep breath and count to ten. I'm not telling you how to handle your physical relationship. I'm simply sharing God's viewpoint on love, sex, and relationships. If you don't like what I have to say, feel free to continue banging the headboards. But if things were going so well for you, why bother asking me for advice?

You're right—I haven't had sex. But I don't have to put my hand in a fire to tell you it's hot, nor do I have fight a lion to tell you it can kill you. According to an old Chinese proverb, "The best way to figure out what is down the road is to ask those coming back." I haven't walked all the way down the road yet, but I've spoken to plenty of folks who are walking back and they have given me much wise advice. More important, I've asked the Creator of the road where it is going, and He was kind enough to write it down (hint: the Bible).

You're right, I'm not an expert. I'm just a fellow soldier fighting in the trenches with you. But when a bullet whizzes by my ear, I'd be doing you a terrible disservice if I didn't yell "Duck!"

—JBI

Dear Jason,

I'd like to say that I've saved myself for marriage, but that isn't the case. I slept with a handful of women in college before dedicating my life to Christ five years ago. Since then, I've met this wonderful Christian woman and am thinking about proposing to her. She has no idea of the type of lifestyle I used to live before we met. She grew up in the church, has godly parents, and has never had sex. How do I approach this conversation with her? Do I tell her all the details of my past or should I just not bring it up?

Dave S.

Omaha, NE

Dear Changed Man,

You have chosen the road less traveled, my friend, and I applaud you. In fact, it is even more difficult to stop having sex once you've tasted the fruit because you know how sweet it can actually be. But you will be blessed for what you are doing.

You certainly have a responsibility to share some of your past with your future wife, but the key word here is "some." There is no benefit to sharing all the details of your past sexual experiences with her—number of partners, names, dates, preferred sexual positions, etc. You simply need to let her know that you have a past. If you pour out all your whipped-cream-and-chocolate-covered experiences with her, you will simply plant seeds of doubt and fear in her heart. You are not the man you used to be. You are a new creation, and you are proving that to her by honoring her body until the wedding day.

But be prepared for her to ask some difficult questions. Just because you have been forgiven of your past sins doesn't mean that there may not be consequences for your actions. If it becomes a big issue between you two, sit down with a marriage counselor and work through it. But be encouraged—you are doing the right thing.

—JBI

Dear Jason,

I'm twenty-eight and I've been having sex since I was twenty-one. I don't just go around and sleep with any guy I can find, but when I get into a serious relationship, I want to share myself with him. I don't have any hard and fast rules, but after I've dated a guy for about six months, I usually think about sleeping with him. What is wrong with that? At that point, we are usually committed to one another and we both enjoy the physical experience. When I find the right guy, I'm sure he'll be thankful that I've had a little practice.

Maria L.
Miami, FL

Dear Practice Makes Perfect,

How is this six-month, verbal-commitment, no-real-guidelines thing working for you? Not too good, huh? Don't get me wrong, I get a burning in my loins after about six months with a woman as well, but I know that once I climb over the vertical limit, the relationship is doomed for failure. The reality is that the six-month mark is of no real significance. It may feel like you are more mentally committed, but you are still just dating.

If you go to a bank to borrow ten thousand dollars, they are going to want some collateral, some guarantee, in case things don't work out and you can't repay the money. The same methodology should be used in a dating relationship. If your boyfriend wants to have sex with you, I'd suggest getting some collateral in case things don't work out. A wedding ring, for example.

Remember, the last couple of rungs on the sexual ladder are incredibly unstable, and you'll be vulnerable to the storms of life. You may want to get a marriage net to put around that ladder before you climb to the top. It could certainly save you if you fall. Just a suggestion. . . .

—JBI

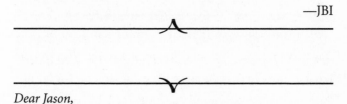

Dear Jason,

This guy I've been dating is a real catch! He is intelligent, dashingly handsome, and very funny. All my friends love him, and I'm often told that I'd be a fool to ever let him go. The only problem is that we don't believe the same things. I think you should go to church on Sundays, and he thinks you should go to football games. He says he believes in Christ, but there isn't much evidence in his daily life. I want to talk to him about it, but every time I bring it up, he just shuts down. So I just let it go. Should I be worried about it?

Barbara G.
Houston, TX

X

Dear Show Me Your Savior,

Houston, we have a problem.

Yes, you should be worried—very worried. In order to build a life together, you have to share a belief system and a set of values. In other words, you need to share the same spiritual foundation. If you remember what we discussed in chapter 3, an unshakeable foundation is poured by building a relationship with Christ and cultivating the fruit of the Spirit. If you don't share these same fundamental values, what do you have to build upon? Similar tastes in music and fashion? Your favorite football team?

He may be a real catch. He may be incredibly intelligent. He may be dashingly handsome. Your friends, family, and dog may love him. But if he doesn't share your deep-rooted passion for Christ, you are setting yourself up for failure. Sure, he may come around down the road, but do you want to bet your life and happiness on that?

Don't think you can change men. Women can't change

men. You can plant a seed of hope and water it, but only God can make it grow. It is better to be considered foolish by your friends than to marry an ungodly man and be considered foolish by the Lord.

—JBI

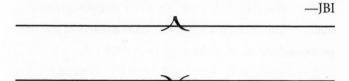

Dear Jason,

My fiancé loves to look at pornography. Since we are trying to wait until we are married to have sex, he says it is his outlet. He has even invited me to go to the strip club with him and his friends a couple times. I haven't agreed to go yet, but I guess it's okay if he looks and doesn't touch, right?

Rebecca J.
Nashville, TN

Dear Peering into Hell,

You're kidding me, right? You don't really believe the garbage that what you see and think doesn't affect who you are, do you? Because what you see and think directly affects your heart and character! All aspects of your life—the spiritual, intellectual, emotional, and physical—are intricately intertwined. The "you-can-look-but-you-can't-touch" idea may be the prevalent way of thinking in today's society but it is a losing strategy. You look at something because you are enticed by it. This enticement breeds desire, and then the desire grows into sin. Sin, whether it is acted upon or not, burrows into your heart and affects all your decisions.

The "you-can-look-but-you-can't-touch" theory is even more detrimental to men because we are visual creatures. We lust with our eyes. That is why pornography is such a mankiller. It allows men to objectify women and sets unrealistic expectations about sex. If your boyfriend is viewing pornography, he is developing impractical expectations about what your sex life will be like when you are married. He is also filling his love-void with lust, an unsuitable and very dangerous replacement. Men who struggle with pornography before marriage almost always struggle with pornography after they get married.

If a "sexual expert" tells you that there is no harm in looking and not touching, it is because he too enjoys gratifying his own lustful appetite. Pornography, by definition, is "imagery intended to provoke feelings of lust in the viewer." Why would a person intentionally place himself in the line of fire? That is just not wise.

If your boyfriend likes to watch women take things off, you ought to let him watch you take off his engagement ring and give it back.

—JBI

———————————^———————————

———————————v———————————

Dear Jason,

I really love this guy I'm dating, but he isn't a spiritual leader. When it comes to going to church or attending Bible

study, he only goes when I constantly remind him. I think he'll
come around once we tie the knot and he sees how important it
is to be the leader of our house. What do you think?

Kendra F.
Denver, CO

X

Dear Tying the Knot (around Your Neck),

Marriage doesn't solve problems—it reveals them. Whatever issues you have when you are dating are magnified a hundredfold when you bring them into the same house. If someone is messy, it may be a little annoying while dating. But clothes strewn all over the bedroom floor will become completely frustrating during marriage. Likewise, a lack of financial discernment may cause a little concern when you have separate accounts, but it is completely unacceptable when he buys a sports car on your joint account.

If issues of personal hygiene and house maintenance are disruptive, imagine how much conflict can arise when a couple doesn't agree on spiritual values and roles in a marriage! The reason that half the marriages in this country end in divorce is because they weren't build upon a foundation of shared values in the first place. If your boyfriend isn't a spiritual leader now, the chances of him transforming into one after the ceremonial kiss are slim to none. In fact, once you have married him, he has even less reason to change— you have already committed your life to him!

If you truly desire a godly relationship, ask yourself this question—Do I love the guy I'm dating or do I love the IDEA of the guy I'm dating? Many of us, myself included, have confused the person we are dating with the ideal person we hope to date. Many people have great Personal Qualities but are still developing Godly Characteristics. No matter how great his Personal Qualities are, he is an empty vessel without a heart for the Lord. And if you marry him, the only knot you'll feel is the noose tightening around your neck.

—JBI

Dear Jason,

I've recently become a Christian and realized I need to stop having sex with my boyfriend until we get married. Unfortunately, he doesn't share my conviction. In fact, he thinks I'm insane and often hints that things may not work between us if we stop having sex. I don't like being torn between what I feel like I should do and what he wants me to do. How do I handle this?

Kathy W.
Des Moines, IO

Dear Convicted,

You're in a tough situation, no doubt. Let me ask you a question—do you think you could enjoy lifelong happiness and experience passionate love with a person if you had to constantly compromise your heart? I didn't think so. But that is exactly what you would be doing if you just give in and give up your body.

Instead of drawing a hard line and telling him that you are not going to have sex anymore, try to share with him *why* you don't want to have sex anymore. Explain your relationship with Christ and how He modeled sacrificial love by denying His own personal desires for the best interests of all people. Explain that the deepest level of physical intimacy (sex) demands the deepest level of commitment (marriage). Because most men's primary love language is physical touch, he is probably feeling rejected since you decided not to have sex. Be very empathetic and remind him that you are not rejecting him—in fact, you care about him deeply—you just don't want to share that kind of physical intimacy until you have a ring on your finger.

The talk may work and it may not. If he truly loves you, he will see that any relationship is bigger than just the sex. But be prepared for him to walk away from the relationship. And if sex is all he wants, you are better off without him. He is missing out on the best part of your body—your heart.

—JBI

. . .

If you would like to read (or submit) more questions about dating, sex, and romance, feel free to check out Jason's Web site at www.jasonillian.com.

11

More Than Happily Ever After
What God Desires in Our Romances

*"Do not follow where the path may lead.
Go instead where there is no path and leave
a trail."*

RALPH WALDO EMERSON

At one of the conferences where I was speaking recently, a gentleman told an engagement story that left the audience stunned. It was a lesson about God's love—in fact, it *was* God's love that just happened to come to us in story form. The audience knew it was going to be a memorable listen when the tall animated gentleman started the story by telling the crowd that he and his fiancée's nicknames were "Sassa" and "Frassa," respectively. *Oh yeah, this was going to be good!*

Sassa said that he dearly loved his girlfriend and wanted to make their engagement something Frassa would never forget. Like most women, she had been trying to downplay the excitement of getting engaged, but Vegas oddsmakers had ten-to-one odds that there was a torn-out picture of a Vera

Wang gown in her purse. To pull off a surprise engagement, he had to play it cool and quietly sneak up on her heart.

Although he didn't reveal how long it had been since the story had taken place, you could tell from the sparkle in his eye that he remembered it like yesterday. Most of the listeners didn't know the speaker particularly well, but it was obvious that he had a heart for the Lord and would be a shoe-in with any family. In fact, he shared that he always thought that speaking to the parents would be the least of his problems. So we were all taken by surprise when we learned that Frassa's family defended their daughter against him like the Texans defended the Alamo. From what I could discern, there appeared to be two major problems—(1) Her parents were churchgoers but held the New Age belief that "all roads lead to heaven," and (2) her parents had her future planned out until she was thirty and he wasn't in the original blueprint.

Because he knew her parents had concerns about the possibility of their marriage, he invited both of them to dinner to ask for her hand in marriage. This was his first major mistake. He said it was like being in a demolition derby without the car. Anytime one parent had a concern, the other one quickly backed it up with five other concerns. Of course, he should have realized that he was in for an Ali-sized beating when he had to call her parents multiple times over a couple of weeks to even arrange the dinner. "But when you are in love," he said, "you are willing to suffer at great lengths for the person you hold dear." Good point.

He prayed that the Mexican dinner would end with a fiesta

and a hat dance, but the plane only continued to lose altitude when Sassa told them *when* he was going to ask for their daughter's hand. "We're going to be out of town that weekend," scowled Frassa's mother, who was quickly starting to resemble a pitbull. She stated her point vehemently as if to warn the young courter that it was not open for discussion. Unfortunately, that was the only weekend that both Sassa and Frassa were going to be in town for a couple of months, and because her parents had taken so long to get back to him, he had already started planning the engagement. He dug deeper to see if they could change their weekend plans. Little did he know that he was digging his own grave.

"We can't just change our plans that quickly, young man," snapped her mother again. "Besides, we already have plane tickets and reservations. We can't throw all that money away." *Mayday! Mayday! We're going down!*

Sassa glanced over at Frassa's father with the words *Help me!* written all over his face. But her father just nodded in total agreement. Sassa had to do something and do it quickly.

"Well, I don't want you to miss out on your only daughter's surprise engagement party just because of the finances," Sassa said. "Just let me know how much the plane tickets are and I'll be happy to reimburse you for them."

Not only were the parents shocked that he had made such an offer, Sassa was shocked that he said it! *Filter, for Pete's sake, filter before you speak!* he thought. He had *no* idea how he was going to pay for two plane tickets on top of the engagement ring and the extravagant party he was planning. Fortunately,

Sassa had called their bluff by realizing that the vacation was merely an excuse to derail his plans, and the parents quickly changed the conversation to avoid promising to be at the party.

The two-hour meeting lasted two days, or at least it felt like it. When Sassa finally waved goodbye to his future father and monster-in-law, he quickly tallied the results of the meeting. *One begrudged blessing. Two furious parents. And three chunks missing from his rear end.* Not the ideal situation, but he had survived. Besides, Frassa's love was worth it.

I figured that things had to start getting better for the poor suitor, but I was wrong. I began searching for a doggy bag when he said that the parents went back and told their daughter about the surprise engagement. I continued to feel lightheaded when the couple's dinner with the parents a few days later ended with them screaming at him and accusing him of being a liar, a fake, and a lowlife. Relief must have been all he could feel when the parents finally stormed out of the room like a couple of spoiled children and refused to support the engagement.

At this point, I don't think anyone would have faulted the guy for dropping everything and running in the other direction. But true, unconditional love is a powerful thing. Instead of panicking and hiring a hit man to off the parents, Sassa rolled up his sleeves and reengineered his plan to make his girl's wildest dreams come true. Because he had less than two weeks before E-day, he had to recruit a number of wonderful friends to help pull it off.

And pull it off, he did. It was unbelievable! Men cowered in their chairs as the standard engagement process was lifted to new heights. Women swooned and imagined being whisked away by equally as valiant a prince. It was a romantic story pulled right off the Hollywood screen. It was the stuff dreams were made of.

Since Frassa's parents had disclosed his previous plans to her, Sassa attempted to use this to his advantage. He flew his family in on a Friday afternoon and invited Frassa out to dinner with them. While enjoying a nice but casual dinner at one of their favorite pizzerias, Sassa received an "emergency" phone call from one of his friends. Of course, it was a carefully planned "emergency" that was all part of the master plan. One of their mutual friends had just undergone back surgery and Sassa was using it as a distraction to get free from Frassa for a couple of hours. He quickly excused himself from the table and told Frassa that he would meet them at the movie after checking on his friend.

In reality, he quickly headed back to his apartment and readied the stage. He lit hundreds of candles around his place, which overlooked a moonlit lake and a sparkling fountain. He pulled out a bottle of her favorite wine and put it on ice. He scattered crimson rose petals all over the floor and placed two roses on the bed where she would be sleeping. He turned on the stereo and placed a tailor-made CD with their favorite love songs on at just the right volume. He then carefully placed two presents that his friends had helped him choose in plain view for her to see. Everything was perfect. He made the call. . . .

"Frassa, I'm sorry but I won't be able to meet you at the movies. My friend is really hurting. Why don't you just have my parents drop you off at my apartment? I'll leave a key for you and meet you there as soon as I can."

She bought it. He sat anxiously at the apartment awaiting her arrival. Although no one knew it, he must have run to the bathroom a hundred times; he was so nervous. Finally, after what seemed like forever, he heard a car drive up and his princess's footsteps echo up the stairs. When her key hit the front door and it opened, all he heard was a gasp.

Shocked and amazed, not expecting him to be there, she tiptoed through the hallway admiring the romantic setting. Because Sassa had carefully orchestrated this playful game of cat and mouse, she walked through the different rooms searching for her love before finding him in the bedroom, holding a single rose. The music began.

She started to cry. Seeing the wine, the gifts, and the extravagant décor, she knew where this was going. He asked if she would be so kind as to grant him this dance. Over the next thirty minutes, they danced, alone and in love, in the middle of the room. They whispered sweet nothings in each other's ears and tried to soak up every minute of this memory. After they finished dancing, they lay down together on the bed and shared a glass of wine. Some moments are too precious to live quickly and this was one of them. They reminisced about how they had met, joked about their adventures, and talked about their future together.

Finally, he pointed to the presents and asked if she would

like to open them. Of course, she had been eyeing the two boxes, especially the little one, for quite some time. He handed her the big box first. She opened the ornately wrapped gift to find a brand-new pair of silk pajamas that she had wanted. He told her that those were for her to wear on this special night. Then he handed her the small box. She opened it very slowly, only to find . . .

A pair of slippers to match the pajamas? A coy smile crept across his face. Catching on, Frassa smiled, laughed, and threw her arms around his neck. They kissed, not for the first time, but for the millionth time that night. After wrestling around the room, Frassa sat up awaiting another little package, hopefully one with light blue wrapping. Instead, Sassa surprised her again.

"Well, it is getting late. You better get some sleep," he whispered, kissing her on the forehead. "We have a big day in front of us tomorrow."

"Oh . . . okay," she stammered, wondering *what* in the world was going on. Where was the big sparkling diamond she was expecting? "Do I need to wake up at any specific time in the morning?"

"No, just sleep in and enjoy yourself. We'll get going whenever we get up and moving." But in reality, Houdini had other tricks up his sleeve.

The next morning, Frassa was awakened by her loving boyfriend and breakfast in bed. In addition to enjoying her favorite bagels, fruit, and orange juice, she had a bouquet of mixed flowers on her tray. Before she could even wipe the sleep from her eyes, Sassa put their favorite romantic movie, *Notting Hill,* on the television and crawled into bed next to her. They ate breakfast, cuddled, and watched Hugh Grant and Julia Roberts struggle through love in a way they would never have to again. The fantasy continued.

As the movie ended, Sassa pulled his sweet girlfriend from bed and said, "I want to show you something." He then led Frassa to the door of the bedroom. When she opened the door, she walked into another dream as if she had fallen asleep again. There was a path of roses leading all the way from the bedroom to the living room. The morning light had illuminated the entire room and she saw dozens of orchids, lilies, and roses surrounding a nest of pillows and blankets. Hand-in-hand, the two lovers walked out into the nest to find a curious scrapbook lying in the middle of all of it. Glancing up at Sassa, Frassa wondered if it was all right to open it. It was. And when she did, she couldn't believe her eyes.

The four-inch, bound Pooh-Bear scrapbook was a near-perfect timeline of their entire dating experience. It had their first movie tickets, numerous flirtatious e-mails, various newspaper clippings, cute love letters, and pictures of the lovebirds together. For three years, Sassa had been quietly accumulating all their memories and organizing them accordingly. If she would have looked down at his hands, she would have noticed that his fingertips were nearly raw from scrapbooking until 2:00 a.m. nearly every night for the previous two weeks. He wanted it to be perfect, and so far, it was.

Once again, she began to cry. He anticipated it and pulled

a box of tissues from behind one of the pillows. She sat down in his arms and they flipped through the scrapbook page by page, cherishing every recorded memory. For over an hour, they laughed and cried, and then laughed and cried some more. When they reached the last page, she swiveled around in his arms so that she was facing him. She planted a wonderful, warm, passionate kiss right on his lips. Yeah, two weeks of scrapbooking was worth it.

After enjoying a few intimate moments, he picked her up and told her to throw on some sweats. They were leaving in five minutes. When she worried that she wasn't dressed properly, he assured her that they weren't going anywhere fancy—there was just a little something that he wanted to show her.

He was lying, of course, and she realized it when they walked into the nicest hotel and spa in the city, looking like a couple of vagabonds. As they waltzed through the sliding glass doors, one very professional attendant said, "You must be Frassa. We've been expecting you." Frassa's eyes lit up and almost began to well up as she beamed at her future husband from underneath her Gap ball cap. He was prepared. He had put a couple extra tissues in his pocket and drew them like a cowboy draws his six-shooter.

For the next four hours, Frassa was pampered. An entourage waited on her hand and foot as she enjoyed a massage, a facial, a body wrap, a pedicure, and a manicure. She was treated like a princess, and after such delicate care, she felt like one too. After a gourmet lunch, the exfoliated and relaxed bride-to-be floated into the lobby to find her prince waiting for her. Sassa got another big kiss—he could get used to this type of thing!

As they got back into the car, Sassa told his beautiful girl that he needed to stop by his office on the way home to pick up some work. Frassa was so enamored and starry-eyed at this point, he could have said that he was going to wrestle a goat in the middle of the freeway and she would have approved. So he steered the car toward his office . . . and toward another surprise. . . .

When he parked outside his office, he suggested that she go up with him. Walking hand-in-hand down the sidewalk, Sassa quickly darted inside a different building, dragging the unaware Frassa with him. Before she could ask any questions, they were inside the most elegant hotel in the city and on the way to the top floor. When the doors of the elevator opened, Sassa handed her a key to a room that said "Presidential Suite." A few seconds later, she was walking on a floor of red rose petals. The entire suite was covered with them.

As Frassa wandered into her suite, she realized that her wonderful man didn't just stop at roses, oh no. There was champagne sitting on ice and her favorite chocolate-covered strawberries calling out her name. When she walked into the bathroom, which was the size of a small foreign country, she found all of her makeup and primping bags. While Frassa was enjoying a relaxing afternoon at the spa, Sassa had run home, packed up all her stuff, and delivered it to this remarkable hotel room.

"Why don't you look in the closet," said Sassa to the

shocked twenty-two-year-old, who was admiring her unbelievable surroundings.

When Frassa opened the closet door, she saw two brand-new dresses, one black and strapless, the other pink and flowery. He then informed her that both of the dresses were hers to keep. She could choose one to wear that night and keep the other one for a different occasion. There were accessories and shoes to match each in the drawers below. The suite was set up for her to get ready for her big evening. Room service was instructed to bring her anything that she desired as quickly as possible. Before he could step out of the door, she threw her arms around him again. She didn't want him to leave. She *never* wanted him to leave.

About two hours later, Sassa arrived back at the hotel looking sharp and dapper in a midnight-black Kenneth Cole outfit. No matter how handsome he may have looked, however, he was simply no match for the stunning beauty who opened the door in a pink dress. She was breathtaking. It took all his strength not to fall to one knee right there in the doorway and express his love for her.

But he waited. Outwardly he was cool and calm, but inwardly a million different thoughts and emotions fought for his attention. He paced the room while she finished getting ready. When she finally said she was ready and walked back into the master bedroom to get her purse, she returned to find him . . . on one knee. In the middle of rose petals. With a tear in his eye. And a little box in his hand. With one hand over her mouth and the other reaching for him, she stood overwhelmed with emotions, trying not to let her mascara run down her face. He too was overwhelmed with emotions, but a great peace washed over him as soon as he hit his knees. He knew he was doing the right thing.

Like any gentleman, Sassa didn't divulge to the audience all of the romantic details that he shared with his soon-to-be wife, but he did tell us that he took his time expressing his love for her. And when they were both crying and there were almost no more words left in his heart, he said, "I don't know what our future holds, but I know that I don't have one without you. . . . Will you marry me?" And in that breath, he popped open the box to show a brilliant, flawless, round, Tiffany's-cut engagement ring—the exact one she wanted. She wept "yes" through the tears and the joy.

The audience began to breathe again, but Sassa just continued. He said, "And then . . ." *And then! There's more?! You have to be kidding me!? This man has already set the engagement bar higher than any Olympic dater can clear, what else could he possibly do?!* But there was certainly more. Oh yes, much more. . . .

After the teary embrace and the passionate engagement kiss, Sassa and Frassa went to a fancy but relatively quiet restaurant to share a delicious seven-course meal. The meal lasted for over two hours, and like young couples in love often do, they missed most of it as they stared into one another's eyes and talked about their future. When they got up to leave, they both laughed at the fact they were still kind of hungry.

Fortunately, Sassa's multifaceted plan had more food at the next stop. Driving across town, they stopped at a well-known Mexican restaurant that was famous for its outdoor patio and pool area. A few carats heavier, the new Frassa assumed they were going to sit on the patio and have dessert. But when she turned the corner, she saw over sixty of their closest friends waiting to share the exciting news with them. As promised, Frassa's parents had boycotted the party, but she barely even noticed as she saw friends from all around the state. For the remainder of the evening, people took pictures, shared stories, ate too much food, enjoyed one another's company, and soaked up the excitement. And Sassa sat back and took it all in. He was as happy as he had ever been.

Without hesitating, he then said, "A month later, we broke up."

Whoa! What?!

Suddenly, what had appeared to be a slice of heaven looked like a patch of hell. Not only did the story change, but the man who was telling the story also seemed to change right before the audience's eyes. The enthusiastic and witty gentleman stared at his feet for a few moments as if to allow himself to become reflective and somber. He was no longer invincible; he was vulnerable. He was no longer Superman; he was Clark Kent.

Have you ever watched a crowd sit in stunned disbelief? They sit motionless, afraid to move, hoping that if they remain still long enough the shock will pass and things will be better again. But some stories don't end with "happily ever after."

Allowing the magnitude of the event to settle in before continuing on, he said something some people will never forget and most people will never understand. He said, "Love *involves* you, but it isn't *about* you." And then a smile crept back across his face . . . and a wave of peace across his heart.

No matter how much we suppress it, there is a part of all of us that wants love to be fair. We want our romance to be about *us.* We want to give love, but we also expect love in return. We will "do unto others" as long as they "do unto us" accordingly. But if our significant other stops loving us in a way that we love them, we will pull away and deny them the fullness of our love.

God's unconditional love doesn't work that way. He gives His feelings, thoughts, and emotions freely, regardless of whether or not we reciprocate. And when we pull away, He lavishes His love on us even more to turn our hearts back to Him.

Unconditional love is not measured in fairness, but in faithfulness. When Sassa broke up with Frassa, he had to watch as she started dating someone else the same week they called off the engagement. He had to gasp as she allowed another man to spend the night at her apartment. He had to listen as her parents relentlessly and heartlessly gossiped about him to mutual friends. He had to endure the persecution as she and friends mocked him in the media. And this was a woman to whom he had devoted his life! A woman for whom he had changed cities and professions! A woman with whom he shared prayers and intimate moments! Was all of that fair?! Of course not.

But it's not about what is fair. It's about remaining faithful—faithful to those you care for and faithful to real love. Although there were fleeting moments when he wanted to drop-kick her dog, he remembered that he loved her completely and that his love was not dependent on circumstance. She didn't have to earn it, and no matter how far she ran, she couldn't outrun it. It was a love patterned after the love he had been given by Christ. It was unconditional.

He had done everything that love required of him—he walked the extra mile to reconcile their differences, he sacrificed his heart while she pursued other relationships, he fulfilled her dreams by orchestrating an amazing engagement, he endured ridicule from her parents, and eventually, he suffered a broken heart. He knew what it felt like to come to the end of himself. And that was when he realized that love was bigger than him. That love involved him, but it wasn't about him. And when that realization hit, he was able to begin healing. His heart was strengthened, not destroyed, by his suffering.

We often default to the clichéd saying that "God is in control" and that there is a lesson to be learned in each circumstance. But God isn't trying to *teach* us something—He is trying to *make* us something. More like His Son. It's not the type of love story that most of us expect to hear, but it's the type of love that we all desperately desire to experience. And since then, it's one of those stories that has always been close to my heart.

And I guess it should be. I always kind of liked it when she called me Sassa. . . .

Passionately Enamored Ever After

My broken engagement was a painful personal lesson that I wanted to share with you to prove one point—God will use *all means necessary* to draw you close to Him. I may have done a good job orchestrating a romantic engagement, but there were many occasions throughout that relationship when I dropped the ball. I didn't make sure we attended church every week or took quiet times together. I didn't have discerning accountability partners to help me make wise decisions. I didn't draw firm sexual boundaries, instead allowing my fiancée to share my house—and even my own bed—from time to time. I made our relationship about us and what *felt* good instead of about what *is* good. It was only by God's grace that we didn't have sex or get entangled in even bigger problems. Because I allowed us to wander away from God and His perfect design for relationships, our romance failed.

But yours doesn't have to. God wants your romance to be more than just "happily ever after." "Happy" is just not good enough. If marriage is an everlasting covenant, don't you want to be ecstatic, overwhelmed, enthralled, love-sick, and a little crazy? Don't you want to dive off the cliff of life knowing that love will either catch you or give you wings? Wouldn't you rather be "passionately enamored ever after"? "Happy" is for people who like watered-down soda and dropped cell-phone calls. It is not for the hopelessly romantic and eternally minded.

You have to be a little out of your mind to fall in love—it isn't one of those things that makes sense. Some people will think you are crazy, and if you are doing it right, you probably will be a few cards short of a full deck. The greatest things in life were accomplished by people who kept the mental wheel spinning long after the hamster was dead: Noah and the Ark, Michelangelo and the Sistine Chapel, Einstein and the Theory of General Relativity, Jesus and the Cross. These people were all madly passionate about life and their calling. And they were willing to walk out in faith, knowing that God had a greater plan for them, a path that others deemed impossible. If you want to be remembered for your great capacity to love, you will have to keep your relationship focused on the Lord even when it seems like madness to the world around you.

You may wonder if this fight to balance dreams and reality, head and heart, faith and culture, is worthwhile. It is the only fight that is. All the other battles in life are mere symptoms of our struggle to embrace unconditional love. Ironically, you can grasp love only by letting it go. When we hold love too closely or too tightly, we suffocate it. Love is only love when it is held in an open hand.

In successful dating relationships, both parties understand that the romance is about undressing their hearts, not their bodies. Despite what we've been trained to believe, sex is not a basic need for survival while dating. At times, sex is actually a crutch. Couples often use it to avoid revealing the more inti-mate parts of their souls—their hopes, dreams, and passions. True romantic love is built upon God's unconditional love, so in order to experience this romance, you are going to have to dig down to the core of what you believe and be vulnerable before both God and your partner.

But when you dig, you are going to realize that you have to go through something. Through the fear. Through the abuse. Through the loneliness. Through the pain. Through the tears. Through the cynicism. Through the pride. Through the anger. Through the despair. When you finally come to the end of yourself—a place very few people ever reach—you will find true, sacrificial, unconditional love.

You are probably thinking, *This type of love you speak of . . . it's impossible!* And you're right—if it is of your own strength, it is impossible. But *all things* are possible with God. The love you are looking for—the place where you will find your heart when you come to the end of yourself—is at the foot of the cross. It was placed there by a Man with blood-stained tears and holes in His hands and feet. And it's free to whoever will reach out and take it.

You'll Know It's Love When . . .

Where do we go from here? Well, that is up to you. A good love story goes on forever and the magic pen of passion never scribbles the same tale twice. Where another book would begin, mine must end. Whether or not I've ever experienced a love this soaring, this moving, this passionate, God only knows. Perhaps I have only imagined it. But my calling isn't to finish this story. The rest of the story has to be written by you as you work through the challenges of love.

I have certainly not said all that is true about love and romance, but all that I have said is true. Relationships, like geology, are the study of pressure and time. And if you want your relationship to be as precious, rare, and brilliant as a diamond, you will have times when you think you can't go on, when you want to throw your hands up in despair, when you want to give in and give up. Don't. God's delays are not necessarily God's denials. Hold on, hold fast, hold out. Your pain will produce perseverance; perseverance, character; and character, hope. And hope never disappoints us.[1] Only through hope do we learn to pour love out over all aspects of our lives. And when you learn to love, you will be loved.

We all struggle with the same things to one degree or another. We are all searching for seamless continuity in our lives. We tend to gather at extremes, hoping, often praying, for balance. But love doesn't behave like a pendulum, taking measured swings at our beliefs; it acts like a wrecking ball, removing all barriers in defiance with the "truth." When a person asks you, "Do you love me?" they are asking, "Do you see what I see? Do you feel what I feel? Do you share the same truth?" When you respond with a "yes," you obliterate the difference between giving and taking, having and needing, life and death. You create an island of certainty in a heaving sea of uncertainty.

The questions of love can't be answered by a Q&A dating book, a relationship guru, a self-help manual, or a nineteen-and-a-half-step personal-improvement program. In fact, the questions of love cannot be answered by anyone but you. Like toddlers interviewing for senior-level executive positions, we are all totally unqualified for the world of romance. Each relationship is new. Each situation is unique. And our prior experience, no matter how diverse, cannot prepare us for the job we are about to accept.

Fortunately, all our experiences, good and bad, help us define the gap where love ought to be. Even though we can't decide when this gap will be filled, we can decide how wide, how long, how high, and how deep that love will be when it gets there.

Wherever you are in your relationship, *be all there.* There is no greater gift. It is where you are meant to be.

"How will I know when it is love?" you ask.

You'll know it's love when she doesn't think she's cute wearing a ragged old pair of K-mart sweatpants and a Hollister T-shirt—and you can't take your eyes off of her. It's love when she calls you "googily-bear," "shuga," or "Pooh." It's love when she turns into a jungle gym around all the kindergarteners at church. It's love when she shouts in a library and whispers in a concert and turns right from the left-hand lane and turns leftovers into an all-right meal and runs when the floor is wet and walks in the hundred-meter dash for success and smiles and laughs and reminds everyone that we are all going to be okay.

You'll know it's love when she rolls up her Cache pants, kicks off her stilettos, and dives headlong across a water-soaked tarp while the neighborhood kids chant medieval water-war cries. It's love when she devours two Jimmy Dean chili dogs at the ballpark while "quietly" telling the pitcher that his mother is a man. It's love when she nearly starts a forest fire trying to microwave a Tombstone pizza. It's love when you gaze at her, step back, and take a deep breath—in awe that such a wonder should even exist.

You'll know it's love when you feel her twitch right before

she falls asleep and when she never remembers drooling on your chest. It's love when she can miss Michael Jordan walking right next to her but spot a three-by-five-inch shoe-sale sign a hundred yards away. It's love when you hear her pray for those who have done nothing but cause her heartache. It's love when she reminds you that our world isn't too big, our dreams are far too small, and our differences pale in comparison to our similarities.

You'll know it's love when she can tell what colors match indigo and plum. It's love when she would rather dive on the concrete and catch the football than let "those overpaid desk-jockeys win the game." It's love when she cares for gay people, straight people, tall people, short people, skinny people, fat people, black people, white people, people without homes, people without families, and people without hope. It's love when you know that if you blink, you may miss her doing something you'll never see again.

You'll know it's love when it is not a pink elephant, we-are-the-world, kumbaya feeling, but rather a calloused-hand, damaged heart, dreams-meet-reality passion. Real love will help untie things that are knotted up inside and tie things that are dangling loose.

Most important, you'll know it's love when you see God in her eyes.

When you feel completely undressed and completely covered at the same time . . . then it is love.

May we all be so blessed as to find it.

Notes

Chapter 1: Completely Incomplete

1 Quote attributed to Albert Einstein (source unknown).

2 1 John 4:16.

3 Esther L. Devall and Jeanne M. Hilton. "Compassion of Parenting and Children's Behavior in Single-Mother, Single-Father, and Intact Families." *Journal of Divorce and Remarriage* 29 (1998): 23–54.

4 C. S. Lewis, *An Experiment in Criticism* (Cambridge: Cambridge University Press, 1961), 18–19.

5 Matthew 5:1–12.

6 See Colossians 2:23.

Chapter 2: Killing Jerry (Maguire, That Is)

1 Blaise Pascal, *Pensees and Provincial Letters* (New York: The Modern Library, 1941).

2 John 3:16.

3 Psalm 46:10.

4 Book of Exodus; Numbers 14:34.

5 Galatians 1:17–18.

6   Matthew 4:1–11; Mark 1:12–13; Luke 4:1–13.

7   Mark 4:34.

8   Qtd. in C. S. Lewis, *The Four Loves* (New York: Harvest Books, 1971), 108.

9   C. S. Lewis, *The Four Loves* (New York: Harvest Books, 1971), 121.

10   ———, *The Problem of Pain* (San Francisco: HarperSanFrancisco, 2001), 91.

Chapter 3: Swimming in Cement Shoes

1   Galatians 5:22.

2   Ben Affleck and Matt Damon. *Good Will Hunting* (Miramax Films, 1997).

3   2 Corinthians 6:14.

4   John Michael Montgomery. "Life's a Dance." *Life's a Dance.* Warner Brothers, 1992.

5   Genesis 1:27.

Chapter 4: Sprinting with an Anchor

1   Genesis 2:18.

2   See Matthew 4:19.

3   Luke 9:3.

4   2 Samuel 11.

5   Erich Fromm, *The Art of Loving* (New York: Harper & Row, 1956).

6   "Born Again Christians Just As Likely to Divorce As Are Non-Christians." The Barna Group. http://www.barna.org/FlexPage.aspx?Page=BarnaUpdate&BarnaUpdateID=170.

7   1 Corinthians 13:4.

8   Jeremiah 17:9.

9   Matthew 28:19.

Chapter 5: Walking Back to the Castle

1   Jeremiah 29:11.

Chapter 6: When Men Are Passive . . .

1   David Murrow, *Why Men Hate Going to Church* (Nashville: Nelson Books, 2005).

2   Judges 6–7.

3   Numbers 14:6–10.

4   Book of Psalms.

5   "U.S. Congressional Life Survey: What Are the Major Challenges That U.S. Congregations Face?" U.S. Congregations, www.uscongregations.org/challenge.htm (26 October 2002).

6   Ephesians 5:21–23.

7   John 13:1–20.

8   Genesis 3:1–12.

9   1 Samuel 17.

10   Daniel 1.

11   Luke 3:23.

12   1 Timothy 4:12.

13   Song of Solomon 2:7.

14   Genesis 39.

15   John Eldredge, *Wild at Heart* (Nashville: Nelson Books, 2001), 9, 16.

16 Angela Thomas, *Do You Think I'm Beautiful?* (Nashville: Nelson Books, 2003).

17 Ephesians 6:10–18.

18 Gary Chapman, *The Five Love Languages* (Chicago: Northfield Publishing, 1992).

Chapter 7: . . . Women Are Desperate

1 John Eldredge, *Wild at Heart* (Nashville: Nelson Books, 2001), 51.

2 See Proverbs 31:11.

3 Shea Gregory. "Confessions of a Sex-Starved Single." *Today's Christian Woman,* www.christianitytoday.com/tcw/2000/001/4.46.html (Feb. 2000).

4 Genesis 1:26, 2:22 (NASB).

5 See 1 Timothy 4:8.

6 John 8:1–11.

7 Matthew 1:18–23.

8 Joshua 2.

9 Mark 16:9.

10 Book of Ruth.

11 John Eldredge, *Wild at Heart* (Nashville: Nelson Books, 2001), 190–192. Thanks for the insight and idea, brother.

Chapter 8: "Meating" People

1 Matthew 14:13–21.

2 John 11:38–44.

3 Mark 8:22–26.

4 Luke 10:27.

5   James 2:18.

6   Song of Solomon 1:7.

7   Genesis 2:24; Genesis 3:16; Matthew 19:4–6, 8; 1 Corinthians 7:10–11; Ephesians 5:21–23.

Chapter 9: Staying Vertical

1   1 Corinthians 6:12.

2   Greg Behrendt and Liz Tuccillo, *He's Just Not That Into You* (New York: Simon Spotlight, 2004).

3   Tony Evans, *Tony Evans Speaks Out on Sexual Purity* (Chicago: Moody Press, 1995).

4   See 1 Corinthians 6:12.

5   Matthew 5:8.

6   Genesis 2:24; Matthew 19:5.

7   Matthew 8:14–15.

8   Genesis 1:27.

9   "The Family Portrait: A Compilation of Data, Research and Public Opinion on the Family." Family Research Council (Washington, D.C., 2004).

10 1 Corinthians 7:1 (KJV).

11 Tony Evans, *Tony Evans Speaks Out on Sexual Purity* (Chicago: Moody Press, 1995), 30.

12 Proverbs 4:23.

13 1 Corinthians 6:18.

14 "The Family Portrait: A Compilation of Data, Research and Public Opinion on the Family." Family Research Council (Washington, D.C., 2004).

15 See 1 Corinthians 6:18–19.

16   1 Corinthians 6:15, 20.

17   C. S. Lewis, *Mere Christianity* (San Francisco: HarperSanFrancisco, 2001), 104.

18   1 Corinthians 6:16.

Chapter 10: More "Buts" Than a Nudist Colony

1   "The Family Portrait: A Compilation of Data, Research and Public Opinion on the Family." Family Research Council (Washington, D.C., 2004).

2   1 Corinthians 13:5.

Chapter 11: More Than Happily Ever After

1   Romans 5:3–5.

About the Author

JASON ILLIAN is a multitalented national speaker, successful corporate executive, and television personality. For the last decade, Jason has toured the U.S., sharing the message that romantic love is built upon God's unconditional love. He has addressed young adults in both colleges and churches, as well as corporations and government entities, including the House and the Senate. He garnered national attention when he shocked pop culture in early 2005 with his refreshing stand on sex and intimacy on ABC's *The Bachelorette*.

With a rare combination of intellect, creativity, and athleticism, Jason graduated Magna Cum Laude from Texas Christian University with a BBA in International Finance and continued his studies with the London School of Economics. He was named one of the top twenty students in America by *USA Today*, was a finalist for the Rhodes Scholarship, and was an NCAA Academic All-American while captain of the TCU football team. After working for a multibillion-dollar investment management firm, Jason started his own executive management company and trained with the Stagen Institute, a nationally recognized transformational leadership institute dedicated to coaching executives and entrepreneurs.

He currently resides in Fort Worth, Texas, and attends Oak Cliff Bible Fellowship, where the Senior Pastor is Dr. Tony Evans.